24 May 96

3 CILGWYN ROW
LLANDYSUL
DYFED
SA44 4BD

01559-362275

Thank you for your letter, your order and your cheque. I hope you will find the book to be interesting reading.

I enclose an order form in case someone else would like a copy!

With thanks

Walter Evans

'EVANS ABOVE ....!!

The Life and Times of an Army Chaplain 1942-1981

Walter Evans
June 1996

The Reverend E W Evans MBE

First Impression—March 1996
Second Impression—May 1996

ISBN 1 85902 317 7

Published by
The Reverend Walter Evans MBE
3 Cilgwyn Row
Llandysul
Dyfed
SA44 4BD

Printed by
Gomer Press, Llandysul, Dyfed.

CONTENTS

Author's Preface

This small book was compiled many years after most of the events recorded in it took place. One reason why it was written was the desire to provide my two daughters, Ann and Ruth, and my grand-daughter, Rhiannon, with some record of the years spent moving around as an Army family.

Since my wife Peggy and I were married, we have lived in 20 different houses, large and small, grand and simple, in many different places. Each has been a home, thanks to the spirit and sense of family we were blessed with.

My best thanks go to General Sir Peter de la Billiere KCB KBE DSO MC* for his very generous foreword to my book at this particular time with his heavy commitments here and abroad.

One or two others have provided much support to the project, and my thanks go in particular to The Reverend J N M Davies MBE, a fellow Army Chaplain, good colleague and wise mentor, who constantly demanded my attention to the project in hand. My best thanks go also to Mrs Joan Wales, a kind family friend, who persevered over the preparation of the text. I am also grateful to other friends for their encouragement, advice and helpful suggestions in finalising the work.

My reminiscences may make a small contribution to the archives of The Royal Army Chaplains' Department, which is 200 years old in 1996. The history of Army Chaplains goes back for many centuries before 1796, for until that date they were appointed by Colonels of Regiments. The history of the Battle of Agincourt (1415) was written by a Chaplain who was present. In the Army which fought at Crecy (1346), three grades of Chaplains were mentioned. Chaplains have been privileged to minister to the fighting men and women of our nation in Peace and War over many generations. All Chaplains have always been volunteers, and 172 lost their lives in the war of 1914-18, and another 96 did not return from the war of 1939-45.

In retirement one has more time, and indeed the obligation to reflect. Some people would say that a Chaplain to the Forces is a contradiction in terms, posed in the question, 'How can you be a soldier and a Christian?'. The Forces do not make wars, but have to carry out the will of their nation, be it right or wrong. It is patent that the role of the Chaplain is to support the Services in their tasks, however difficult and unpleasant they may be. I was faced with the question above in 1942, when I was about to become a Chaplain myself, and the answer is made plain in Chapter 1 of this book. 'Onward Christian Soldiers'—a hymn which is hackneyed and overused, is nevertheless not without its teaching. As I have seen it for myself, there have been occasions in plenty where a Christian presence is expected, and indeed demanded. Someone once said, in a lecture to Chaplains—'Never forget that the sole job of the Chaplain is the soul job'. Men of the SAS have described the need as 'professional integrity'—that is what they expected and wanted from their Chaplain.

Towards the end of my ministry in the Forces, I had the privilege to be the Chaplain to The Royal Hospital Chelsea, where 400 or so old soldiers spend the evening of their days in peace and reflection. Many are the words of wisdom I have heard there, and in turn I have tried to apply them to the review of my own career.

Every year the Moderator of the Church of Scotland makes a formal tour of the Forces, and when I was at Chelsea, the Moderator of that year came there too. He came on a Friday, and joined in the weekly Service for the sick Pensioners in The Infirmary there. He told me afterwards that he felt that his experience that day was the most moving he had met in all his travels, if not in his whole Ministry. He said he felt a very special sense of admiration for their lives in service, rendered with but little reward, and that now they were able to live in the remainder of their lives in the peace they had spent their own lives in attaining.

For a variety of reasons, military persons are a very conservative group of people, and do not lightly display their feelings on faith and fear. As an Army Chaplain I have lived alongside so many who have learnt so much comradeship, felt so much apprehension and insecurity, and yet have found a spiritual strength in so doing, whilst the busy world does not really know or understand.

Over the 200 years that the RAChD has been in being, and in the generations before, there have been many whose work has not been recorded anywhere, whose feelings and actions have remained unknown. It is because of this that I have felt that one or two thoughts of my own may have some bearing and insight into what may seem as a conflict, but which in fact is not, in the matter of Soldiering and Christianity.

For myself, I have learnt that Chaplains will always depend very much on the support they are given by All Ranks in the Army, their families and friends, who realise what Chaplains stand for, and respond accordingly. In return, I have learnt that a golden rule for Chaplains is ever to remember that 'Nothing is too much trouble, and everyone is worthwhile'; that all Ministry is Service, rendered in the name of our Lord Jesus Christ.

Foreword

by

Sir Peter de la Billiere KCB KBE DSO MC*

This is the story of a special Padre in every sense of the word. Walter Evans was one of the most battle experienced Chaplains to serve in the Army after World War Two with operational service in North Africa, Italy, Belgium, Germany, and then to Malaya, Singapore, Borneo, Kenya and Oman. He survives as the most loved and respected of Padres amongst the post war Special Air Service and at fifty-five accompanied them on operations in Oman.

This is a human book and what it lacks in pomposity and conceit it makes up for with the Author's humility and love of mankind whatever the individual's faults.

His personal account, so full of anecdotes, amusing, sad or happy, but all quintessentially human, brings out the importance of the Chaplain's role in supporting Service Commanding Officers. In time of war and peril the churches are full but in the security of peace when men are too busy or self-conscious to get to Church then the Padre must take God to the men. As Walter Evans so penetratingly demonstrates 'behind every household door there lies a problem'.

It is my experience that a good Padre is the conscience of the Commanding Officer and the patron of the men. Certainly this description fits Padre Evans.

Moral courage is a greater challenge than the physical. Walter Evans possesses both but excels at the former. This is a book for all creeds and for non-believers: it brings a shaft of light to the reader's life.

Chapter 1

The shape of things to come....

I was born on 2 August 1916 at my Mother's family home at a village called Eglwyswrw in Pembrokeshire, but after a few weeks, came to Lampeter, in Cardiganshire as it then was, and lived there until I left home at the age of 23.

Educational facilities were good at Lampeter, and after Primary School, I went to the school attached to St David's College, Lampeter, and hence in 1933, I entered the College itself to read a degree in Honours History. St David's University College, as it is now known, has, since my days, become part of the University of Wales, and now flourishes as never before. Being a local boy, I lived at home, which was fortunate for many local lads who graduated there. Fees in those days were met by scholarship grants (if lucky), and the efforts of one's parents, which usually meant great financial sacrifices. My only Brother, two and a half years my Junior, and I were both fortunate in this respect, and I have to this day, a sense of gratitude and appreciation to my late parents for their dedication and efforts to make the best of the opportunities available to us.

The death of my mother, at the early age of 50, from cancer of the liver, was a severe blow to my father, my brother, and myself. She was a very noble, upright and Christian character who did her best at all times to give us the benefit of her dedication and inspiration in all that she did.

She was taken ill about Christmas 1931, and within 12 weeks she had passed away. My father was in business in Lampeter, and during her illness I stayed at home from school for a whole term to help my father to carry on and care for my mother. I was studying for the Higher School Certificate (today known as A levels) at the time, but never sat for the examination. Fortunately I had obtained the Oxford School Certificate with 8 credits in 1931, and later in 1933 sat for a Scholarship to the College, and was awarded one for my first year's studies, and also in each successive year as they came along.

To lose one's mother when my brother and I were 13 and 15 respectively gave us both a great sense of loss, but which loss we were unable to appreciate fully,I am sure, as I reflect in later years upon it. Later on my father remarried, a widowed lady who was in fact a (distant) relative, and she was kindness itself to us both, and a great comfort to my father, when we were both away during the War. She died in 1946 not long after the War was over, and we missed her greatly too.

The College was founded in 1827, as the result of the efforts of Bishop Burgess of St David's Diocese, with the intention of raising the standards of education of the Clergy of the day. Long before the University of Wales was visualised, the College at Lampeter was granting BA and BD degrees by Royal Charter, and as such was the only college of its kind and status, outside the ancient universities.

In my own case, I was brought up in the Church, attended the local Parish Church with Services in English and Welsh. I was also a Choir Boy (of indifferent quality), and as such a member of the Parish Church Choir when the Archbishop of Canterbury came to Lampeter to preach at the Centenary Service of the College in 1927. My motives for being ordained seemed to follow a natural progression for after my Degree, I continued at the College to study Theology in preparation for Ordination.

My old College had to battle for about 20 years to get into the Universities Grant Scheme, but won out in the end. The Principal was a very able man, Canon J R Lloyd Thomas MA, with a lst class Honours Degree from Lampeter, and who wrote the book 'Moth or Phoenix' which tells the whole story. In the book he makes clear that as a priest it was not incumbent on him to "blow his own trumpet" in the matter, but for others to say what they think. This is the point I would offer about this publication too.

Contrary to popular misconception, the College was never a church institution, and never had a test of orthodoxy and belief at any time. In the course of its long history, it suffered many ups and downs, and more than once was threatened with closure. One of these crises occurred after World War I, and was only overcome by the appointment as Principal of Dr Maurice Jones, the Rector of Peppard, a Jesus College Living near Oxford, and a distinguished ex Chaplain 1st Class in the Royal Army Chaplains' Department. He was born at Trawsfynydd, a fluent Welshman, and from a very poor home. A great orator, he became an Army Chaplain in 1890, served in the Boer War and many stations overseas. He retired in 1915, before the age limit of his class at that time. It is said that this was in protest at the ruling at the time, in the thick of World War I, that Senior Chaplains were based in the UK, and not allowed to proceed to the front in France!! He was an ebullient character, a militant, military Chaplain, and during his 15 years as Principal of the College from 1922—1937, he put the College "on its feet" again. He "sold" it by preachments up and down Wales, and anywhere else where he could invite himself. He also encouraged and fostered a small but steady flow of Lampeter men into the Services (particularly so to the Army), as Chaplains in the years between World Wars I and II. The records of the Royal Army Chaplains' Department will show this. The persistent but amusing claim that the Department has been run by (if not for) Irishmen and Welshmen may have some backing in the story of Maurice Jones. He retired as Principal of the College in 1937, at the age of 75. He was offered a lump sum payment of £2,000, or an annual pension of £300 a year. Being an old soldier, he opted for the pension, and drew it for about 20 years, before his death in Wimbledon, London, at the age of 96, in the late fifties.

Every Lampeter Graduate of that era had reason to know of the existence of RAChD, even if he had no ideas about becoming a Chaplain himself. This was the background, if you like,to World War II, so far as the College was concerned, and it was to affect dramatically the lives of so many who studied at Lampeter, myself included.

A Wartime Ordination ....

I graduated at St David's College in June 1936, just before I was 20, with a second class Honours Degree in History. By 1938, I had passed (with a little difficulty) Parts 1 and 2 of the General Ordination Examination. I spent the last year, before I could be ordained (at the statutory age of 23) as Assistant Master at St David's College School, in the grounds of the College, which School I had attended as a boy.

War broke out on 3 September 1939, and some of the clergy in the Diocese of St David's had already been mobilised, either in the Territorial Army or RARO. Others were earmarked to leave for the Services as and when required, and the Bishop was taking every possible step to provide replacements for the gaps as they occurred. It was duly arranged that I should be ordained Deacon on St. Matthew's Day (21 September) and "serve my title" (first curacy) in the parishes of Narberth with Robeston Wathen, Pembrokeshire. Then came the snag—I could not be accepted by the Rector of the said parish because my predecessor there, the Reverend W H Reid, had not yet left for the Army, which he was earmarked for. The Bishop, however, found himself able to deal with the problem of Ecclesiastical Law by an ingenious solution put forward by my late Mother's Uncle, The Reverend Canon D A Jenkins, Rector of Cellan with Llanfair Clydogau near Lampeter. He had no curate but was prepared to offer me a Title (non-stipendiary) to enable the ordination to proceed, which in due course is what happened. All went well, and I was licensed to the Curacy of those Parishes by the Bishop, on the day of my Ordination.

Within four days, however, it was "all change" again, for Reid received his call-up papers, and left Narberth immediately. I was then licensed again, this time as the proper, salaried Curate of Narberth with Robeston Wathen, having received two Ecclesiastical Licences within ten days! There was an unusual follow up or follow on to this matter. The Rector of Narberth at that time had one only son who had taken a degree in Theology at Oxford in June 1939. He was at Ripon Hall, Oxford when I reached Narberth, doing his post-graduate training for the ministry. His father was in some concern about the situation, and feared his son might be called up for General Service very soon so the Bishop was asked to ordain the son as Non-Stipendiary Curate in his Father's parish, which ordination took place at Advent 1939. So now there were two curates at Narberth, and I felt that as soon as I was priested (September 1940), I should move on to allow the Rector's Son to became paid curate to his Father. (The comment here could be that there is nothing new in the Non-Stipendiary Ministry which we hear so much about these days).

The whole of South West Wales at that time (like everywhere else) was full of servicemen of all sorts, especially after the 'miracle of Dunkirk' in May 1940. Narberth was full of Royal Engineers of the 53rd (Welsh) Division from the day I started there. Very soon I was involved in a vast canteen, run by the Parish Church, in a large, vacant building owned by the local brewery. As a side light on life there at this time, I tell how I was in Haverfordwest, the nearest town, one day, visiting a barber's shop for a haircut. In the barber's chair, under the barber's robe, I was unidentifiable as a local clergyman. Who should come in but the manager of the local branch of the bank at Narberth, where the canteen account was held. He had obviously had a very full and jolly lunch and he was soon giving a full account of the affairs of the canteen in the parish. (It should be said that everything was sold at rock bottom prices—mainly tea and cakes—but the demands were obvious and the proceeds kept increasing). Anyway—it was a very embarrassed Bank Manager who recognised me when I emerged from the barber's chair!! On Christmas morning 1939, I was going early to the first service of the day at the parish church, and I met on the way a young, brash enough, 2nd Lieutenant (TA) of the Royal Engineers, and it seemed to me a case of his thinking "better a morning after than never a night before". There was no one about, and when he came up, he leered at me and said "Where are you going, Padre?" I replied that I was on my way to church for the first service on Christmas Day. His reply was (and I have never forgotten it, from my impressionable youth) "Do not expect to see me there—I am a bloody heathen".

I cannot say that I was in any way upset or otherwise put out over his remark. What I will say is that I have what I think is a retentive memory and this remark was 'saved' if one can use an information technology expression. I thought to myself that I would use that incident at some future date, and tucked it away in my memory, and in my little book of life's incidents, which little book has been an invaluable reminder as the canvas of life unfolds.

Those were the days of Church Parades, and I well recall hearing (later on) of the Chaplain whose Regiment was fairly foul-mouthed, from top to bottom, so to speak. One Sunday morning, he began his Address and went on solidly for ten minutes with a swear word as every other one in his talk. After a minute or two of this, the Regiment was aghast at the performance in Church, and thought he had gone mad. And then, he stopped suddenly, and said "You are all horrified at hearing this in Church, aren't you?—now you stop it, outside." And for months afterwards, seemingly, there was never a swear word heard, at any level!!

I moved to the town parish of Cardigan in September 1940, where I remained until I joined the Army two years later. Like a good many of the younger clergy, I was keen to go as soon as possible, and my aim had been September 1941 (after two years in Holy Orders). However, as the Bishops had to countersign every application, and some Bishops were somewhat loathe to release too many too soon, I had to wait until three years were up from Ordination, before I was allowed to leave.

There were others in my position in my Diocese, and we all knew that for various reasons, release to the Forces had to be planned, to some extent anyway. As I remember I was given a promise at the end of two years, and I was expecting it to be honoured, as it duly was, in due course. Cardigan, 1940—42, was equally full of servicemen, but in this case, they were mostly visitors from the very busy anti-aircraft practice camp at Aberporth, a few miles away. There was also a small RAF station, which operated tiny, pilotless, aircraft, "Queen Bees", which towed targets for the Army Gunners Practice. I particularly recall the Adjutant of the RAF station, an ex-serviceman of World War I. He had great musical talent, and a wonderful voice, and ran great concerts at the camp. However, he would never sing in a camp concert on Sundays—he considered that his gift belonged to God on that day, and he would sing sacred songs at any church which asked him. He was known for miles around, a great Christian of strong convictions.

The Headmaster of the local Secondary School at Cardigan commanded the local Home Guard (Dad's Army), and I was soon in it as some sort of Intelligence Officer. They were busy, hectic, days and nights, for I was also for a time in the ARP Organisation, as an Ambulance Driver, with a large saloon car, converted to take four stretchers in case of need. Night after night we were summoned to our posts by the Air Raid siren, and could see Air Raids on places like Swansea and Pembroke Dock, as well as listen regularly for German Raiders bound for Belfast or Liverpool.

Early in 1942, things began to move for me. I was asked to attend for interview at HQ Western Command at Chester. I was seen there by an Assistant Chaplain General who originally came from Porthcawl in Glamorganshire. His clerk, in an outer office, turned out to be a Welsh Lance Bombardier whom I did not know, but came from near my home. His claim to fame as a clerk to Chaplains seemed to come from the fact that he was by way of being a Methodist lay preacher in the villages of Cardiganshire. When I passed through his office on the way out from "the presence" he invited me to sit down for a few minutes. Presently, he said, a chit would come out from the Assistant

Chaplain General saying "yes" or "no" to my application. Within ten minutes of my interview, I knew that I had been accepted, and this was confirmed by letter within a few days. Shortly before I left Cardigan I was walking down a street one day, with my Vicar, the great Canon Hamer. We met the Minister of the Welsh Congregational Chapel, who had with him, his Chapel Treasurer, an ex- Merchant Navy Ships Engineer who had been twice torpedoed in World War I. The Minister tackled me, and said that I should not be going to the Army, that my place was there with my people. To which I could only reply "and who will be with my people's sons and daughters, wherever they may be?" The ex-engineer then said "You go, young man—you will be twice the man when you return"—end of conversation. The Minister was very sincere, very much a pacifist, but I think he was mistaken, as I understood it, at my age.

Some of my contemporaries in the Church in Wales, for their own reasons, felt that their place was in the parishes where they were stationed. Every Service Chaplain is a volunteer, and in all our history Clergy have never been called up for Military Service. I was young (26 when I became a chaplain), fit so far as I knew, with no 'encumbrances'. I was quite sure, then and since, that I had made the right decision, and in those days, a firm decision was called for, without too much ado.

The old Bishop's Palace and the Cathedral entrance at St. David's in Pembrokeshire.

Chapter 2

Join the Army ....

I was ordered to report to the (wartime) RAChD Training Centre which was located at the Teachers' Training College at Chester, the teachers having vacated the premises for the duration of the war. We were to arrive on Friday, 25 September 1942, and as it happened, three of us, whose homes were in the same street at Lampeter, were on the same intake, HB Hughes, CCD Lewis and myself. We set off together by bus to Llanwrda and then caught the Central Wales line train to Shrewsbury for Chester. (No private transport possible in those times). By an extraordinary co-incidence I took my daughter Ann to the same College, to the same entrance door, for Teacher Training, exactly 25 years later, on 25 September 1967!!

The Intake Course was short and sharp, of 14 days duration. It was run by The Reverend Canon HS Astbury (who was in fact the Principal of the requisitioned college) and the Reverend Ronald Sinclair, both Chaplains in World War 1, together with some outside instructors.

The Brothers Woods, sons of the then Bishop of Lichfield were both there. Frank, later Archbishop of Melbourne was back from the Middle East, to take over as Commandant, and his Brother, Robin (later Dean of Windsor and afterwards Bishop of Worcester) was there on the Intake Course with the rest of us Lectures filled a crowded programme, one only on each of the many subjects. One, I well recall, was on Map Reading, based on three questions. "Where am I?", "Where are they?" "How do I get there?". The wits used to say it was easier to ask than puzzle it out! The lecture on the NAAFI stressed the importance of Chaplains making sure they cared for the staff of the NAAFI—"The servants of those serving"—Survitor Servientum". In later years of service I always tried to do this, and I well recall the gratitude of managers and manageresses in that they and their staff were not forgotten—souls like the rest in our care.

Masses of notes and proforma were handed out, as was inevitable a crash course of that sort. I recall that among them (and I still have it) was the duplicated form of Service for the Burial of a Jew. Someone said "This is a mistake" only to be told, "No, you keep it with you—you may need it in some situation that may come up one day". True enough—months later, in Italy, I buried four soldiers of my Regiment, one of whom was Gunner Liebovitch, a Jewish Tailor from the East End of London.

All denominations (except RC) were represented on the course, and the total number was about 40. Years later, when Warden of our own depot, I looked again at the course photograph and realised that one of its members had been killed in action. 96 chaplains died in World War II, out of about 3000 who served in the Army. A rough calculation would show a death rate of about 1 in 30, considered by those who know these things, to be a high proportion. This in turn leads to the point that unarmed, non-Combatant Chaplains "bore the burden and heat of the day" with everyone else.

On every course a Chaplain was detailed, in turn, to say Grace at a meal. On the last night it turned out that it was Robin Woods turn to do so, and he began by saying "I will say Grace in the way my Father used to say it". He duly said his Grace, and on sitting down afterwards, was asked by a young Welsh Baptist Chaplain sitting opposite "Tell me, who is your Father then?", which created a great ripple of amusement.

As I remember it, we were not asked as to where we would like to be posted. Postings in those days were not 'matters for discussion' as they seem to have become in more recent years, in the piping days of peace. In due course, towards the end of the second week, a list of postings was put up on the notice board. Two of us, Robin Woods and myself were posted to North Wales District, Robin Woods to Kinmel Park, Rhyl, and myself a place called Coed-y-Brenin Camp, for Trawsfynydd Practice Camp, Royal Artillery, and Harlech Anti-Tank Range. There was one other posting to the District, namely HS Astbury, the departing Commandant of the Centre, who took over as Deputy Assistant Chaplain General (Senior Chaplain) of the District itself.

The first posting ....

We all left, amid some trepidation, early on the Friday fortnight, after 14 days in the Army, and I found myself with 184 (Army) Field Regiment, Royal Artillery, at Coed-y-Brenin Camp, a few miles north of Dolgellau where I was met off the train. On seeing the Commanding Officer, Lt. Col. A.N.S. Corbett, I was informed that my predecessor had left for overseas, earlier that week; that he had been there for six months, that he had the great facility of remembering everyone's name and background without any difficulty at all. That was to be my aim in turn. I found out why he found it so easy when I discovered that his name was H E Jones, a year senior to me at Lampeter, Senior Scholar of his year, who graduated with a lst class degree in History. No wonder he could remember names as he did!

I soon settled in, for everyone was very kind and helpful, and with the use of an Army motorcycle I soon found out the extent of my "parish". The winter weather was very cold, fuel was in very short supply; one day a week there was a complete ban on transport, except for the mail truck and ration supplies, and the turnover of personnel was very high, because of constant postings. Trawsfynydd was a huge, busy, training camp, known to generations of gunners as "trousers", since its origin in 1907. Nowadays all traces of Army occupation are gone, and its claim to fame is a nuclear power station which is itself closed and its re-opening somewhat unlikely, for safety reasons. Harlech was an anti-tank practice camp on the dunes near the sea, now the site of a golf course. There was little or nothing in the way of church furnishings anywhere in the camps, and I remember borrowing a cross and candlesticks and a few other items from the Vicar of Maentwrog, a village on the Harlech road. He had been a curate at my home town of Lampeter just before the war.

Long days on ranges, evenings at canteens, and some weekday as well as Sunday Services were the pattern of life there. There was once a dance at Dolgellau, organised by the Regiment, which I duly attended, with everyone else, in uniform, with me in my clerical collar. I recall seeing there a group of local men, members of the Home Guard (Dad's Army again). As I passed near them in the hall, one of them said, in Welsh "who the devil is this?"—obviously referring to me, the first Army Chaplain he had ever seen. I stopped and said "I speak Welsh, as well as you do, so please let me explain who and what I am!!!". The reaction was hilarious all round. One other incident, of a more serious nature, occurred at this camp. As we were in a very hilly, indeed mountainous area, a piece of flat ground for football was at a premium. One day, the Second-in-Command, a somewhat overbearing type, as he knew that I spoke Welsh, told me to accompany him to go to see a local farmer. There was a reasonably flat field there, and the farmer was an elderly man who spoke no English at all. He was obviously a bit frightened of the army and its ways, and the Second-in-Command's manner did not help. I was to tell the farmer, in Welsh, that this officer was going to use his field, without by your leave, for games of football for the Regiment. I was not at all happy about the Second-in-Command's attitude, and when the old farmer told me that the field was ear-marked for oats, I had the answer. I explained to the old man that all he had to do was to tell me that he was reporting the whole matter to the County War Agricultural Committee (who controlled all food production), and then sit back and let them get on with it. I duly told the Second-in-Command that the farmer's intention was clear enough to me. He was very cross, but he knew he had no rights in the matter at all, and there was nothing he could do or say. The Army never got the field, for food production was far more vital!

After Christmas Day 1942, I was given eight days privilege leave, and the standard advice was to take it when offered; come another day and there could be no leave to worry about!! I went home by train to Lampeter on a Monday morning, and on the following Thursday went for the day to Cardigan, to see one or two friends there. About 1400 the local police found me, and told me I was to report back to my unit at once. My home at Lampeter had been rung from Coed-y-Brenin Camp, and I guessed that it meant an immediate move for overseas.I went back by the first available train (next morning) and by that night I reached Uttoxeter, in Staffordshire, to join 79 (Hertfordshire Yeomanry) Heavy Anti-Aircraft Regiment, Royal Artillery. They were based on Uttoxeter Workhouse, and told me I was to go on 14 days embarkation leave as soon as I had a medical examination.

My posting was not unexpected. We had all been told on our Intake Course that normally one could expect a first move after three months, usually for overseas. Hundreds of people were being moved about every day of the week, and the arrival of a posting order did not really worry me at all.

The Medical Officer, a veteran of Delville Wood, France, in World War 1 ('I was there') examined me and said I had flat feet. (At my original examination before joining, at Aberporth Camp near

Cardigan, flat feet were mentioned but never much made of). I duly went for a medical board to an Army Hospital at Lichfield.

In the corridors there I met a young doctor (Lt RAMC), who was as unlearned in the ways of the Army as I was. He asked me what I was there for, and when I explained, he said airily "come with me—we will soon sort that out". He took me into a side-room, examined my feet, and said "That is fine—you will be all right as you are". I duly went back quite happily to Uttoxeter, and took a train to Lampeter that evening, for my 14 days embarkation leave. I reckoned to be home next morning, all being well.

At Cardiff Station, about 3 am, my name was called out repeatedly on the loud speaker system. On reporting to the RTO (Railway Transport Officer) I was told to return immediately to my unit. When I got back to Uttoxeter, I was met by a truck and a furious message from the Medical Officer to the effect that when he had ordered a medical board for me I was to *have* a *medical board*, and no nonsense.

I was taken straight to Lichfield, saw and passed the Board, and then taken straight back to the railway station at Lichfield again! (Incidentally, flat feet never have bothered me, before or since!).

It was of course dark by the time I was on my journey home for the second time within 24 hours. All the compartments were darkened, with a dim blue light in the ceiling as the only illumination. Opposite me in the compartment was an obvious farmer, who lived somewhere near Crewe. He immediately started a conversation by saying 'I see you are a Chaplain. Tell me, do you believe in an after life?' As he was a complete stranger, I began to wonder for a moment whether he was going to throw himself from the train, or do some drastic thing. He went on to say that he had buried his wife 18 months before; that he never went to Church but that his Vicar was his best friend. He then said 'I have been forced to the conclusion that there was either something or nothing, and that further more that there cannot be nothing so far as my wife was concerned'. He said that he had come to a cross-roads about it all, and he would have to change his posture completely. For the little time we had before he left, we then had a warm, friendly conversation about the meaning of life and the Church.

My 14 days leave went all too quickly, and in the usual way of these things, I remember very little about it, except that my very kind Step-Mother was very concerned about my Brother and myself. My

Brother had volunteered for the RAF from College in 1941, before completing his training, and was already in the siege of Malta, where he spent three years in all.

When I returned to Uttoxeter, I began to find out who was who. The Regiment was commanded by a Regular Army Officer, Lt. Col. A B de C Dickinson RA, a clergyman's son, who did everything possible to settle me in. This was very reassuring to me, because I had a lot to learn, and what I did learn became the basis of good relationships wherever I went, at that time and also in years to come, in various other postings in the Army. A good CO (I never had a poor one) knows what to do with his Chaplain and Medical Officer, who were both 'attached' personnel from separate Corps of the Army. General de la Billiere, British Commander in the Gulf War 1992, in his book 'Looking for trouble' has something to say on the subject. Everyone else, except for perhaps three or four pre-war soldiers, were either Hertfordshire Yeomanry Territorial Soldiers, or men called up for "the duration of hostilities". Everyone was very kind, and from that date in January 1943 until the Regiment was disbanded in January 1945, I was their Chaplain, up hill and down dale, through good days and bad. The Assistant Adjutant, an Aberdonian named Harry Slater, took me under his wing, and I learnt all about Army administration very quickly from his guidance. We still see each other regularly, and have done so over a period of 50 years now. He had an excellent career after the war in the Home Civil Service, and now lives in retirement in London, where his family doctor, until he, in turn, retired also, was our Doctor in the 79th for nearly two years, Victor Dellal by name.

Chapter 3

Overseas... Afric's Sunny Fountains

As it transpired there were very few days left in Uttoxeter, and one dark January night, we all entrained at the local station for an unknown destination, over a thousand strong.

Most Servicemen going overseas in such circumstances tend to keep their innermost thoughts very much to themselves. It all comes out later, I found, because at the time censorship and secrecy were the first essentials. There was no great sense of excitement; rather one of what lay ahead is something of a closed shop. A kind of one day at a time attitude prevailed. Boredom came later, and even that did not worry some people too much; as a Regiment we had one suicide only during the whole of the North African and Italian Campaigns. For myself, I liked people of all sorts, and found this a great asset to my own well being.

After an all-night journey with drawn blinds and dimmed lighting, we found ourselves next day at Gourock, the 'tail of the Bank', near Glasgow. The whole place was teeming with shipping and activity of all kinds, and during the day (20 January 1943) we embarked aboard the Union Castle Liner 'Dunottar Castle' of 15000 tons. There were about 3000 from various units on board, so that there was very little space anywhere. When you think of package holidays today (50 years on) you can but marvel at the organisational skill that got us all there—thousands of people in the large convoy of ships, and 'packaged' us all in somewhere. As I recall it, we embarked on a Thursday, and I soon found out I was the only Chaplain on board. (I believe there was a War Office ruling that Movements and Chaplains always had to make sure somehow that every ship had one chaplain on board as it left our shores). We pulled away from the quay side to the jeers of the Royal Navy's ships' companies—"off you go—the Royal Navy will fetch you back"—a reference to Dunkirk of 1940.

Next morning I began to think of how I could possibly manage to arrange some sort of Sunday Service, and I duly went in search of OC Troops and the Ship's RSM, who represented the Army's permanent staff on board—who did trip after trip overseas. Neither was very helpful to me, and merely said (quite incorrectly really) that Divine Service was nothing to do with them, and that I would have to see the Chief Officer of the Ship, somewhere on the Bridge above.

There were signs everywhere 'out of bounds to all ranks' and 'crew only' etc. etc., but eventually I got to this very important person, the Chief Officer. He truly was a great man, and immediately put me at ease in his cabin. His name was Sowden, a practising Christian and good churchman from Yorkshire.

He told me exactly what to do, and how to do it. He suggested Holy Communion in the Ship's lounge at 08.00 (occupied at night by a mass of men sleeping on the floor). 'I will be there' he said 'and everything will be ready for you'. The ship, as a peace-time liner, had Prayer and Hymn books, a portable altar, piano etc. and a steward who knew exactly how to get things together. 'Then' he said 'I suggest you hold two Morning Services at 10.00 and 11.00, one for A & B decks, one for C & D decks, so that all who wished to do so, could attend, again in the lounge. He said he himself would play the hymns for the Services, and read a lesson if I wished him to do so. I ventured to ask him who would want to fill the lounge twice over. "You wait and see" he said " you will find the place packed—they will be there all right, if they are going off to war!" Finally, he suggested hymn singing and prayers, at 20.00 in the evening, and he would play if necessary.

True enough, it worked out exactly as he said, on the two Sundays that we were aboard his ship. Attendances were excellent, the ship's inter-com having created the necessary publicity. The Chief Officer also told me that he never left the Bridge at all, except for meals and Church, during the whole voyage, so grave was his responsibility. He told me that I was the ship's chaplain for the voyage, that I was to go wherever I wished to on board, without fear or favour. In particular he asked me to visit the crew at their work stations, and finally said that in spite of OC troops and fearsome RSMs, and sundry Commanding Officers, that <u>he</u> ran the ship, and his words and wishes were law—and rightly so. I was to answer to no one but him, and I had his personal 'carte blanche' in every way. It was evident to me that the ship's Chief Officer was very experienced in Trooping, which was the liner's role at this state of the War. He was a Churchman and he used the Chaplain he had on board for the voyage, in what he thought was the right way.

I was very glad of the chance to be of service to him, the crew of the ship, and all on board, and I had a busy ten days whilst I was on board.

I was to use his cabin on the bridge if I wanted to prepare a sermon, or get prayers and readings ready, or read quietly as he knew how cramped every space on the ship was. If I needed anything while I was there I only had to press the bell and his personal Steward would see to it. Because of the fact that the North African landings were in the charge of the American Army, all ships were completely 'dry' and no one on board got an alcoholic drink at all, except the chaplain way up aloft on the bridge, where I had a whisky once or twice during the voyage!

I went to see him before we disembarked at Algiers, after what proved to be a ten day voyage, uneventful apart from one or two sharp scares. I wanted to thank him particularly for his kindness to me, and he then told me that he lived his (very perilous) life with a complete sense of trust in God. During the voyage, no one had undressed at all (except for boots at night), because of the risk of torpedoes. The convoy had sailed across to New York, almost, and then back across the Atlantic to Gibraltar. Every day we could see the same neighbouring troop ships, a large number of them, escorted by naval craft of various kinds, darting to and fro like sheepdogs guarding a flock of sheep. The speed of the convoy was slow—in fact the speed of the slowest sheep, as it had to be!

I never saw the Dunottar Castle again, but I know the ship survived the war, as I saw the name several times in the years post war, so I can presume that the gallant Chief Officer survived as well. It would have been nice to know how things went for him, and lots of others I met in all sorts of places, but it was such a transient life, and one could never keep up with every contact made in such situations. For one thing, censorship was very strict, and no one could keep lists of names and or addresses in such circumstances, for security reasons. Wars today seem to be very different, what with satellite communications, and the hungry media always at one's elbow!

Chapter 4

British North African Forces—The First Army...

We arrived at Algiers on 1 February 1943, early in the morning, and disembarked immediately. This was a firm ruling, always imposed, and it came back to mind in 1982 over the Sir Galahad tragedy in the Falklands. It has been claimed that some units there stayed aboard somewhat longer than they need have done.

We did not leave the docks at all, but re-embarked that same day, in the afternoon on board "The Royal Ulsterman" (a cross channel boat from the United Kingdom to Ireland). As the dusk fell, we were off again, so as to travel as far as possible in the dark, before arriving at Bone, in Tunisia, next day. The move was done on a "light scale" whereby everyone moved in what he stood up in, plus big and small packs. Kit bags and heavy baggage was to follow "as soon as possible". Again, in the Port of Bone, which had been severely damaged in the initial landings, we disembarked as soon as possible and marched about 5—6 miles to Bone Transit Camp, near the airfield, outside the town. There we were to wait in company with many other units, for kits, guns and vehicles which were in other transport, slower ships. I think I was probably one of the lucky ones, who had packed a spare set of underclothing and shirt in the big pack. I say this because we slept on the ground for three whole weeks before any more kit arrived. The weather was very mixed, the camp was very muddy most of the time, and everyone was getting dirtier all the time. However, in due course, we managed to get a sort of bath (a shower in Bone about once a week, and so a bit more clothing was very welcome).

The chief need of all present was news from home, and we had to live with the fact that letters took six weeks at that time, which was very frustrating for those who had left home with problems behind. Accommodation and food was very simple, as the previous paragraph infers.

When the first mail did eventually arrive, about the beginning of March, about six weeks after we left the UK, there was some excitement, some interest in local news provided, and some instances of grief and sadness. From the beginning of our time in North Africa, I noticed that a few had no mail at all, and I got into the habit of having a word with these people who had no correspondents at all, at some point within a few days. Some were completely indifferent to the fact, because they were loners, for one reason or another. Some on the other hand eventually got a letter infrequently, because those they knew were poor letter writers anyway. The Assistant Adjutant, with whom I shared a tent, and who was my guide and mentor, received with his mail, a letter from the Minister of his Church of Scotland in Aberdeen, a Mr Rankin. In it he gave Harry the news that his father had passed away, very suddenly, while we were on our 10 day voyage. The letter was a very moving script, for he wrote 'You will wonder, Harry, who will lead you in the days ahead, when so much unknown lies before all of us.' Harry was very touched by this remark, and following, when he wrote 'It will be your father and your father's God.' I remembered it too, when he showed me the letter, and ever since have held the Church of Scotland in the highest regard. There were one or two others who had sad or disturbing news of various kinds, and who were always ready to talk about things. Of course, as time went on, there were lots more instances, for many persons in the Regiment. The camp was a vast one, with many units and chaplains coming and going. There were one or two Anti-Aircraft Regiments of our own 12 Anti-Aircraft Brigade, the Newfoundland (Field) Regiment, Royal Artillery, and lots of Line Regiments of Infantry. Life was very basic, and I did see there one day a soldier doing field punishment, shackled to a gun wheel.

There were some strong protests at this, and I never saw it happen again anywhere. I took it that security in any other way was impossible in the situation we were in, and that was why it happened thus. I never knew the name of the unit concerned. Eventually the news was received that my unit's stores had arrived in the theatre of operations, less one Battery of Guns and some small vehicles which had been lost on a ship that was torpedoed on the way out. This meant that two batteries out of three had four instead of eight guns for a while, and people like the MO and myself had to share vehicles for a few weeks. I was offered (and used) a 500cc motorcycle (BSA) as a temporary measure, and this was fine except on Sundays, for very soon the glass cruets in the Field Communion Set were smashed in the pannier bags of the motorcycle. The CO then ruled that I was to have a vehicle and driver all day on Sundays.

There was one very amusing incident during my motor-cycling days. After a few weeks, it was announced that all vehicles in the Regiment had to have a full inspection by the technical arm that knew all about them, and one day all the motor cycles were paraded for the purpose. The Staff-Sergeant from REME, who carried out the check, eventually came to mine, at the end of the line. He had a great big form for the purpose (it was just like an MOT), and the last box on the form was entitled General Condition. Knowing the machine was mine, he solemnly wrote down 'If Cleanliness is next to Godliness, you've had it'. Everyone heard about this, from the CO downwards, and it was a great laugh at my expense.

Our active deployment took place at Philipeville, now known as Skikda, Algeria, and about 60 miles west of Bone, where we mounted an anti-aircraft defence of the town and very busy port. It was a very bustling sort of place, with large reserves of men in camps, as well as complete Brigades of Tanks and Guns resting in camps in the woods around, waiting to go East to the fierce fighting in Tunisia. The General Reserve and Training Depot (GRTD) and the Infantry Reserve and Training Depot (IRTD) were both there, and very crowded at times. There were in addition the 67th and 100th General Hospitals (of 1200 beds each).

RHQ of our Regiment was at first on the town racecourse, and everyone lived for a while on and under the Grandstand. As Army billets went, they were very comfortable, and everyone thought we were on to good things when we saw all the fruited orange trees around the track. We soon discovered that in fact they were Seville oranges, by which time the resourceful old soldier who was Captain Quartermaster (ex World War 1) had the cooks busy making marmalade, and very good it was too. The 3.7" heavy anti-aircraft guns, (16 out of 24) were deployed in troops of four guns each, all around the area.

At that time they were fairly static, which made visiting by the Chaplain and informal services very possible and welcome, as they were always in remote places. I set myself a standard whereby I aimed to give every Detachment a service of 30 minutes duration every Sunday, allowing for 30 minutes between to move to the next position, and 'setting up' again. The result was often a series of eight or nine services on Sundays, and sometimes one or two on weekday evenings as well.

They were very well received, if only because really everyone was always there anyway, and it mattered not what time of day a service was held. On looking back, and learning lessons, I think sometimes that if I had arranged fewer services on Sundays, and stayed longer at each position (perhaps having Holy Communion regularly as well) the results would have been more meaningful.

On the other hand, one great advantage of going regularly to each site, was that you were expected. In those situations where no one left any camp site very much, and there were constant "stand-tos", the Chaplain's visit and Service was very much a part of the week's life. Of course, in addition to Services, I regularly visited two or three sites every day and spent long periods in conversation and visitation in a true pastoral sense.-Early on, I started having a sort of retiring Collection at the Services, mainly because the Regiment was basically a TA Regiment from Hertfordshire, and there were many causes of local interest, notably the hospitals (before the days of NHS) which they liked to support. Hospitals were local, voluntary efforts, and such places as The Watford Peace Memorial Hospital were always very pleased (and proud) to hear from their local Regiment overseas. The sums sent were not large, but they were meaningful, and most gratefully acknowledged with interest and gratitude. I recall once a collection for Barnado's Homes being supplemented by a donation of ten shillings (quite a sum for a soldier) from a Bombardier A-, who was originally a Barnado Boy. He asked me to tell Barnado's of his gift, and imagine his delight when weeks later we had a reply wherein they said that he was clearly remembered, as the Warden of his particular home had been informed and had perused the letter I sent with great interest.

Hymn singing was very simple, very basic, (no pianos—no bands—no tape-recordings as we have today). The Regiment's last active service station in the UK had been at Swansea, and there were many lads from that area in the Regiment, some of them very good singers, which helped a lot for the more popular hymn tunes.

Our first casualty in North Africa was a Bombardier C- who was married to a girl from Neath near Swansea. He was knocked down and killed in the main boulevard at Philipeville. The circumstances of his death were somewhat mysterious until some expert work by a young military policeman Lance Corporal found that both the vehicle and driver were from our own Signal Section. The driver was duly convicted by Court Martial of dangerous driving and sentenced to a term of detention.Records in my possession tell me that there were 102 Communicants in the Regiment at Services of Holy Communion held on and around Easter Day, 25 April 1943. On 29 May 1943, six confirmees were presented for confirmation at the Eglise Reformee at Philipeville, together with others from neighbouring units. They were confirmed by The Rt. Reverend G V Gerard MC Senior Chaplain and Bishop to the New Zealand Forces in North Africa.

Sickness was a big factor of life in North Africa, because Algeria was ridden with Malaria. There were other diseases as well, of course, notably dysentery and sun-burn, but Malaria was far and away the main problem. The French, who had been in Algeria for generations, had done little or nothing about Malaria, but because of the urgency of war, the British Army made tremendous efforts to contain the problem, and deal with the mosquito—infested marshes and waterways. Hygiene sections of the Royal Army Medical Corps were very busy, and their efforts produced very good results in due course.

Because, as an Anti-Aircraft Regiment, "stand-tos" at night were commonplace, it was inevitable that many cases of malaria should occur. I recall that at one stage in Philipeville, I went one week to seek out 150 (out of our approximately 1000) who were hospitalised, mostly by reason of the malaria problem. It took me three whole days to seek out and visit every one of them, a pastoral reward in itself. In one tented ward there was a Sergeant of the Regiment, in the next bed to a young merchant navy sailor, rescued from a torpedoed ship, lost in the Mediterranean. I spoke to him as well, of course. Later the Sergeant told me how impressed this young sailor had been that the Army's casualties received regular visits from their own Chaplain.

I felt I was just doing my job without demur, and was happy as always in doing it. I felt myself to be part of the team, and by this one means the Regiment. The Unit is always the strongest formation in the Army, where people felt they belonged, in a very close-knit fellowship, if one can use such a word. This was especially true in a Regiment like mine, some of whom had known each other from school days in Hertfordshire. The cap-badge worn has always been a great bond, and historically has always been the bonding factor of the soldier's life.

S. David's Day 1943, spent in Philipeville, was celebrated by a service in Welsh, held in the already-mentioned Eglise Reformee in the town. The attendance was excellent, due to publicity in Unit Orders. Later on, in Bone in Tunisia, the Welsh speaking Methodist Chaplain of the North Irish Horse (The Reverend E M Hughes), together with myself, held a monthly Welsh Service on Sunday afternoons in the YMCA followed by Tea and Sandwiches (Char and Wads). The response was tremendous from Units all around, and many an unexpected happy reunion was achieved by brothers, cousins and friends. The gregariousness, and love of singing of Welshmen far away from home, meant instant success for the venture.

79 HAA Regiment, Royal Artillery, was moved back to Bone, after about six months in the Philipeville Area, that is, about September 1943. The North African Campaign had been over since May, Sicily had been invaded in July, and the landings at Salerno, in Italy, had just taken place. About the time we arrived in Bone there was a tremendous (secret) Court Martial there, of about 180 men from various units. They were alleged to have mutinied at Salerno purely because they had received an unfulfilled promise that they would, on discharge from hospitals, be posted back to their own Regiments. On discharge from hospitals they went first to the Infantry or General Re-enforcements and training depots. Unless they managed to find out somehow, and very quickly, where their own Regiments were, they were liable to be sent anywhere, as part of the general re-enforcement system. The system could not wait for or always follow up postings to all sorts of units in all sorts of locations.

The Regimental System for the Infantry is one of the strongest bonds of the British Army, which accounts, understandably one could well say, for the situation which arose. It has been said, many times, by military historians, that the strength of the system was its finest feature, contributing everything to the comradeship and morale of the British fighting man.

One day, whilst at Bone Prison (Civil) taken over for military use, I was told that four sergeants lay there under sentence of death, over the alleged mutiny. All were eventually reprieved and allowed to 'soldier on'. There were 180 convictions in all, but in every case the eventual outcome was a reprieve. The subject was made into a programme on Radio 4 in the late 70's, as a feature which aroused grave disquiet among many who knew something of the facts, and as they were interpreted in 1943-44.

Just before this volume went to print, a new book was published (Mutiny at Salerno. An Injustice exposed. By Saul David with Foreword by Ludovic Kennedy. Brassey £19.95) It describes the experience recorded as shocking reading, and relative to the Salerno events.

As mentioned before, during the whole of my time with 79 HAA Regiment I shared a tent with a young officer from Aberdeen, a Classical Scholar at the University there. He was first Assistant Adjutant of the Regiment and in due course was promoted to being the Adjutant.

He taught me, very quickly a great deal about Army Administration. For this I was very grateful, because it helped me a great deal later on in my career, when I was given more responsibility and seniority in the structured life of the Army in various situations. One of the things I have always remembered is that the importance of knowing all the answers to questions asked is sometimes very difficult, and the true art lies in knowing where to look for them. I always found that the key people in any unit, normally always the busiest in any situation, were always glad to help. I learnt the wisdom of the adage that if you urgently need to achieve something, the really busy person is the one who will get things done.

Eight members of the Regiment were presented for confirmation 1 January 1944, at a service taken by The Rt. Reverend Robert Simpson, Bishop of Southwark, and held at the Eglise Reformee, at Bone. Almost exactly a year later, two out of the eight confirmees were killed at our RHQ, by a bomb which had to be jettisoned by one of our own fighter-bombers, near Rimini in Italy. I knew the two men very well, and saw them every day. I wrote to the widows of both, and eventually heard back from them. They were very grateful for my thoughts, and the part I had played in their lives before their deaths.

Chapter 5

Central Mediterranean Forces.......
'Neath a Blue Italian Sky'

The Winter of 1943-44 was spent in and around Bone, traditional home of S.Augustine of Hippone, as it was originally known, and having many associations with Christianity in the days of The Roman Empire.

In March 1944 we made preparation to move to Italy, and once again dwelt in Bone Transit Camp, with a little more comfort this time. It was on Good Friday, 7 April 1944, that we marched to the Docks where we had landed 13 months before, and embarked on a Dutch troop ship. We set sail that night, and arrived at Naples Harbour very early on Easter Day, 9 April. It was a hive of activity, with Mount Vesuvius active as well. There were three or four Chaplains on board this time and we were told that if we wished to hold a Service of Holy Communion to mark the great Christian Festival, it would have to be at 06.00, as disembarkation would begin at 09.00. Word went round everywhere, and a large number turned up to make their Communion, from the various Units and Services on board.(There was a strange sequel to this, because on Easter Day 1974, 30 years on, I mentioned the occasion in my Easter Day Sermon at The Royal Hospital Chelsea in London. A lady in the congregation became very upset at what I had said. It transpired that the last letter she ever received from her boy-friend, killed at Monte Cassino a week or two later, was a letter in which he said he had made his Communion on board a troop ship in a harbour in Italy at 06.00 on Easter Day).One reads in the Bible about 'casting bread on the waters and finding it after many days.' This was an example of the way in which contacts made are contacts renewed many years later. There was a sadness about this story, and the lady concerned grew close to us as a family as a result of my words on Easter Day 1974. For me it was one more illustration of the fact that 'people matter', and that a long memory is a most useful asset in life.

At about 10.00 on that Easter morning, the whole Regiment paraded on the quay-side, and we marched through the crowded streets of festive Naples (the celebration of Easter, on the very day itself), to a Transit camp at a place called AFREGOLA, to the North East of the city, and a distance of 14 miles. Someone had a nice sense of humour perhaps, in ordering that the very last two in the column should be the Medical Officer and the Chaplain. Dr. ("I was there, at Delville Wood") Woods and myself were put there to deal with those who fell out, presumably. All went well, except for poor old Private Davies of the Army Catering Corps, who really had dreadful feet. We carried his pack and his rifle and lagged behind a bit, to get him to the end of the journey. Private Davies was very sore-footed after the march, but he stuck it out and was able to 'soldier on' as a Cook, doing his dailywork very well. I think he was very grateful for the assistance the MO and I were able to give him that day.

Our stay at Afregola was a very brief one, as our equipment was already in the country, sent out ahead of us. We were swiftly deployed around the great airfields surrounding Foggia, near the port of Bari on the Adriatic Coast. They were very busy days for the Royal Air Force, and we were there to protect them from German counter attacks. The RAF were regularly bombing the oilfields of Rumania and the industries of Czechoslovakia.

Our RHQ was at a village called Canosa, north of Bari, near a small port called Barletta. Hospitals in and around Barletta, the 71st and 73rd, with others at Bari, were very busy places at this time. During my visits to them I saw girls from Yugoslavia, fighters in the Underground movement against the Germans, many of them serious psychiatric cases, due to the mental stress and anguish of their campaign. As these words are written, one thinks again of that unhappy country, torn apart now by Civil War amongst ethnic groups who have lived together so uneasily, ever since the country was 'thrown together' after World War 1.

At this time in 1944, the battles of Anzio and Monte Cassino were raging, part of the strong German resistance in front of Rome. However, in June 1944, just when D-Day was launched in France, Rome fell to the Allies, the Germans having retreated and declared it an open city.

A certain amount of local leave was permitted by this time, and three of us, with a driver, managed to get to Rome for six days. On arrival, the vehicle was put away in a guarded compound, and we walked everywhere on foot! Young and fit, going around Rome as pedestrians was no problem, and we had a very instructive stay, thanks to the erudition of my Aberdeen friend and it has all stuck in my memory ever since.

Because Harry Slater was a Classics Scholar, he knew a lot about Ancient Greece and Rome, and his knowledge was especially helpful to us as tourists in The Eternal City. The Pope held an audience every day at 12.45, especially for the Forces, and gave the traditional blessing in many languages, including English.

After about two months at Foggia, in August 1944, we moved north, through Rome, to provide fire-power for the American 5th Army, who were operating on the west side of Italy, in parallel more or less, with the British Eighth Army on the Adriatic side. We got to a place a few miles south of Livorno (Leghorn), where we stayed a few weeks. The Germans were being driven northwards at this time, but were by no means finished. I recall going from here to Pisa, of Leaning Tower fame, the day after it fell (the city not the tower!) and soon afterwards we got to Florence and Sienna.

Late one Sunday evening returning to RHQ from taking a Service a few miles away, I came across a truck bearing the insignia of the South African Division, with a South African driver and three friends, who were obviously very lost. They turned out to be Engineers, and had come down from the line with the body of one of their number, for burial somewhere. I arranged for them to stay the night at our HQ, and led them the next day to an American Cemetery, a long way back south, where I duly buried their comrade. I wrote to his parents and it turned out that he was the only child of a Bank Manager at Windhoek, South West Africa (now Namibia). I had a very tearful, heart broken reply to my letter and for several years afterwards, I heard from them at Christmastide, enclosing a small gift. It was about this time, while stationed there, that four of our Gunners, returning to a Battery Location, took a lift on top of a 1 ton water carrier vehicle. Half full, they are the most dangerous of vehicles and when this one had to swerve to avoid a donkey-cart with no lights in the dark, the weight of the swirling water inside caused the vehicle to overturn, and all four were killed. One of them was a Gunner Liebovitch, an East End Jew, and this was the occasion when I needed, found and used, the Order of Service for the Burial of a Jew, given me in 1942 at Chester.

These burials took place in the same American Cemetery as the one where I had buried the South African. American Cemeteries then as now, no doubt, were the most elaborately arranged affairs, by comparison with our own arrangements, at least in the initial stages. The cemetery was in the charge of an American Lieutenant, a Top Sergeant, one or two other American NCOs, plus a team of about eight Italian POWs who were the grave diggers. Instead of being interred in the traditional British blanket, each body was placed in a canvas bag, after all ten fingers had been finger printed six times each. One set of prints was put in a hermetically sealed phial in the armpit of the body, one given to myself, and the other four to British and American Records of various levels, including the Pentagon itself. The arrangements probably had to do with the fact that American personnel were never left buried in enemy soil, but repatriated to the USA itself, if the relatives so wished.

Of recent years, Great Britain has moved in this direction too, for repatriation from the Falklands War was a ready option available for the burial of those whose next of kin so wished it. Alternatively, immediate relatives are now offered the opportunity to visit the grave of the deceased, and the scheme (operated by the Royal British Legion on behalf of the Government) provides one opportunity for next of kin to visit the graves of those lost in World Wars. Not all those who were lost in the Falklands War were repatriated and it puts one in mind of the lines, which refer to generations of British dead overseas

"Winds do not blow
Waves do not beat
Where rest not England's dead"

(Over a gateway to a cemetery on an island near Zanzibar)

At about this time, the role of the Regiment was changed, whereby the guns were no longer so much required in an Anti-Aircraft role, and were deployed as Field Guns looking towards the Gothic Line where the Germans were digging in for a hard winter, in more senses than one. It was in September 1944 that Lance Bombardier AG Thomas, the Commanding Officer's driver, was killed by a mortar fragment whilst waiting for the Commanding Officer, and standing in the lee of a house. The Commanding Officer had talked to me more than once about burials, and (rightly) had decided that he would not attend them as a rule, because if he managed to attend some and not others, it would seem improper. This burial of his driver was an exception, as he had been the Commanding Officer's personal driver since long before the Regiment left the United Kingdom.

In October 1944 we received orders to move from the US 5th Army front to the 8th Army front, at Rimini, on the Adriatic. In due course we found ourselves in a place called Cesenatico, about five miles north of the town. By this time, I had been for a week to Assisi, to attend a Chaplains' Retreat. A school for chaplains had been established there, and in charge was none other than Robin Woods, son of the Bishop of Lichfield, who had been on my intake course at Chester in 1942.

It was a refreshing, stimulating, week in one of the great spiritual centres of the land. We were all well and truly inspired by the thought that we were in the home of S.Francis of Assisi, and certainly made the best of our few days to see the Churches and especially the little church of S. Francis inside a larger one, in the valley below the town. I cannot recall that we exchanged experiences a great deal. I think that those present felt that no one else was really interested in what their particular Unit was like. In addition, we were all security conscious, and we knew very little of what the 'big picture' was really like. Some did a good deal of reading, as there were some books available and worthwhile. As our own material was extremely limited, it was a great opportunity to read and ponder something new and substantial, within the limits of our stay of four days.

Fortunately Assisi was in no way damaged by the retreating or proceeding armies, a tribute to the fact that its riches of Christian culture were over and above the machinations and demands of the war.

The great value of our stay there together, about 25 in number, was that it did wonders for our sense of isolation which we all were victims of, to a greater or less degree. We met more often as the war passed to its termination, but in the early days of the campaign I hardly ever saw any other chaplain, except occasionally, by chance, at one of the military hospitals.

True, there were circulars and various pieces of correspondence from 'Chaplains' at Army HQ and General Head Quarters for the theatre of war we were in. A scheme of assistance and training for ordination candidates in the army was started, by means of correspondence courses. It was run by The Reverend Dr. S.G.F. Brandon, DD, a chaplain based at Allied Forces HQ.

The idea was that Chaplains in the field should become

correspondents for six to eight ordination candidates, and there were scores of them in units all over the place. One of the names I was given was that of a Captain in the Oxfordshire and Buckinghamshire Light Infantry, whose name was G D Leonard. I never met him at all in those days, but did so eventually when he became Bishop of London in 1981, and I was at the time Honorary Chaplain to the Lord Mayor of London of the Year. I expressed the hope to the good Bishop that he was happy with his New Testament Greek, because I had not been of great assistance to him in the Field in Italy all those years ago!!

Also, at this time, a Leave Centre for All Ranks, was established in the hill town of Urbino, about 80 miles south of Rimini, and inland from Pescaro. Chaplains were detailed in turn to spend seven days there, on leave-cum-duty, including Sunday Services for those in residence there. My turn duly came, but I had not been there more than three hours when I received a signal to return at once to my Unit, as I was needed there urgently.One of our RAF aircraft, on an airfield down the road, had suffered engine trouble on take off; had tried to jettison its bomb (one only) on the beach nearby, but unfortunately our RHQ building was hit and four soldiers (Royal Artillery and Royal Corps of Signals) were killed instantly. I duly buried them all together at a military cemetery which had been established at Cattkolica, south of Rimini.

It was a time of great fluidity and change. By June 1944, many of the Anti-Aircraft Regiments had been diluted, and in due course it became the turn of the 79th. A number of Gunners were posted to infantry battalions (usually as a group, to one unit). Their places as "Gun Numbers" were taken by Basutos of the Pioneer Corps. The idea was that they could perform certain tasks of the gun-teams, and on the whole they proved very competent. We had a company of them, commanded by a British Captain, with their own Warrant Officer and Senior NCOs.

Some time after they arrived, and were fully operational teams, one of their number went out of camp one night, when he should have been on duty. He duly appeared before the Battery Commander for his offence, when he was ordered seven days confined to camp, on the evidence of the Basuto Sergeant, whose name was Ned. The Basuto soldier then made the strange remark that he would shoot Sergeant

Ned. After the hearing, he went to his tent, got out his rifle, and went to the Sergeant's tent. There he promptly shot Sgt Ned through the neck. The Sergeant was very lucky, for the bullet missed his carotid artery, and in fact did him no great damage. However, the bullet passed on, and killed the NCO in the next bed. Meanwhile, the errant Basuto Gunner had gone straight back to the Battery Commander's Office Tent to tell him that he had shot Sergeant Ned, as he had said he would.

He was immediately arrested, and in due cause he was court-martialled. He was found guilty, and the penalty was death by shooting. He had set out to commit murder, and a death had taken place as a result of his actions, even though it was not the death the soldier he had intended. The proceedings were confirmed in due course by the Commander-in-Chief, Field Marshal H.R.L. Alexander. The Commanding Officer of the Regiment was a very sensitive man, and duly upset, but the Regimental Sergeant Major, said he would cope all right, as he had attended two such melodramas before, once in World War 1, and once in the Army of Occupation afterwards. It was laid down by higher authority that the Regiment itself would carry out the execution. (The Americans sent all their condemned back to the prison in Naples, to be dealt with by an execution squad there). The Basuto soldier spoke no English, and he was a Roman Catholic. So the Roman Catholic Chaplain of the Brigade and myself went to see the "A" Officer at the Brigade HQ, who was dealing with the matter, and insisted, somewhat to his chagrin, that the execution be delayed until the only Sesuto-speaking RC Chaplain in Italy had been located and sent for. He duly arrived, after about three days, from the South of Italy somewhere, stayed the night, said mass in Sesuto with the condemned man before the execution in the morning after.

He was shot in a field near Cesena at 06.00 by ten of our own British Sergeants. They had been summoned to RHQ the night before, to stay the night, and carry out their unpleasant duty before they returned to their own locations next morning. One bullet among the 10 rifles was a blank, so that they could not think that they had personally fired a fatal round.

The whole of this drama was a great upset for the Regiment, because with an old Territorial Army background, they were a very close knit body of men. They had soldiered together, a good many of them, since long before World War II, and in some instances they were walking in the footsteps of their forbears too. The title of the Regiment, The Hertfordshire Yeomanry, was a very proud and ancient one, a title which was justly revered in the Regiment.

However, within days of the events of the execution of the Basuto soldier, the news was received of the complete disbandment of the Regiment. One by one, in descending numerical order of seniority, Regiments of Heavy Anti-Aircraft Artillery were being done away with, and their personnel drafted elsewhere, as the needs changed, and as the war progressed. No one expressed very strong views about it all, so far as I knew, and any form of trauma did not appear. In fact, during the whole of my time with the Regiment, only one man suffered any mental disarray, and one other committed suicide. He was a very quiet, reserved individual, unmarried, who came from Hertfordshire, and no one was able to explain why he had done it. After it happened, I for one, thought his parents should have been told exactly what had taken place. It was, however, decided, to save his parents any deep concern and upset, that it could be recorded as 'Died on Active Service', which was true as far as it went. My view was that eventually, somehow, they would know the truth, and it was perhaps better for them to know it then, than to hear it after the war, in some untoward way.

Many, many years afterwards, when I was living in Swansea, my wife and I were in a big store in the town, and came across a salesman wearing a Royal Artillery tie. I got into conversation with him, and it turned out that he had served in the Regiment when it was stationed in Swansea. He had married a local girl, and because of an accident, had never been with the Regiment overseas. It further turned out that he was a member of 246 Bty, in which Bombardier S.... had been. I asked this person if he knew the Bombardier, and his reply was 'Oh yes, I knew him. I heard in a pub after the War that he had committed suicide'. I should add that the suicide took place sometime before the murder, and there was no possible connection between them.

There was one very interesting exception to these procedures. The 9th Heavy Anti-Aircraft Regiment was a Territorial Army Regiment raised in Ulster, and even in 1944, was still largely composed of Ulstermen. There was no conscription in Northern Ireland, only TA volunteers. They had been embodied as a Regiment in September 1939, and their commitment as such, was for five years only. So, all of a sudden, in September 1944, the whole unit was pulled out of the line, and all who claimed the five year rule, were sent back to Northern Ireland to be demobilised. Many decided to 'soldier on' instead, for the duration of the war, and thereupon signed up as such.

It reminds me of the strange, so unrealistic, system in World War I whereby many Chaplains from parishes undertook 12 months Active Service. At the end of their contract, they left the mud of Flanders for home. How many accepted these terms is not known to me. What is known is that 172 chaplains lost their lives in World War 1, and 96, just over half that number in World War II. This represents a very high ratio, in both Wars, of those who died from amongst those who served. "May they rest in Peace". In the Second World War all Chaplains, like everyone else, had to serve for the duration of hostilities, which made far more sense, and made the contribution of chaplains worthy for the tasks they were given.

Chapter 6

Vale....

Over a period of about eight weeks, covering December 1944 to January 1945, postings arrived for all and sundry in the 79th (Herts Yeomanry) Heavy Anti-Aircraft Regiment. To note a Regiment disintegrating in this way was not a happy experience for any one in it, for the bonds and friendships made were very strong. Day by day stores were handed in, vehicles sent elsewhere, and parties of all ranks left for unknown destinations. Eventually, it came to be my turn, and on 25 January 1945 I was posted, with vehicle and driver to 56 Heavy Regiment, Royal Artillery, which happened to be quite nearby, at a place called Russi. Chaplains belonged to a "pool" and were attached to regiments as required. Gunner Williams, my faithful driver, though originally in 79th HAA Regt, was also in the "pool" by now, and together we left one morning, on quite a short journey. I had been with a company of 1000 plus men who were all known to me—and I had many close friends among them. There was nothing one could do about it, and one had to adopt a spirit of 'off with the old, and on with the new'. That is not to say that one did not regret the parting, and to this day I have the connection with one or two. Some Regiments went in for Annual Reunions after the War, and some survive very well. The 79th did not do this, but my next unit, 56 Heavy Regiment still does, and I have contacts there which are still valid.

56 Heavy Regiment was a set up of really heavy guns, half being 7.2" British Guns, and the other half 155 mm American Guns. The Regiment was part of Two Army Group Royal Artillery, and its fire power was enormous, in support of the lst Canadian Corps, then serving in Italy. Later on, and in post-war literature, the Regiment became very well known because, though unknown at that time, serving in it was none other than "Spike Milligan", one of the original "Goons" and a comedian of great ability. His books about "How I won the War" etc. have been widely read for their interest and comedy.

It was a very noisy Regiment for its shelling was constant and heavy, day and night. Moves of batteries and troops were frequent, because of enemy counter moves.

I recall staying a few nights in a farmhouse, sharing a billet with the Regimental Medical Officer. The old farmer used to come to see us every night and say "buona sera", "buon reposo"! and "buona notte"— "good evening, good repose, good night".

The Commanding Officer of the Regiment, like my previous CO, was a regular officer, and I recall that the Adjutant had been in peace time, the catering manager of the Berkeley Hotel in London. It so happened that one of the cooks at RHQ, an Anglo-Portuguese, had also been at the Berkeley Hotel. The Adjutant and the cook had a brief conference every morning to discuss what had arrived in the rations the night before. As a result of this discussion, nothing was wasted, there were fresh rock cakes every day about teatime, and there was a faint air of the Berkeley Hotel in the presentation!! Life moved on relentlessly, and within six weeks of my arrival, there were rumours (soon to be confirmed) that the Canadian Corps was to pull out of Italy, and be redeployed in the South of France, rejoining its parent formation, the Canadian Army, very much engaged in the battle of the "soft under Belly" of the German Occupation Forces in France. About eight weeks after I joined 56 Heavy Regiment, Royal Artillery, they were gone, the only British unit with the Canadian Corps, and I was once more very much in the "pool" of chaplains together with Gunner Williams and our truck, which was our "mobile" home.

I was sent for by the Assistant Chaplain General 8th Army, to see him on interview at his caravan at 8th Army (Main), now positioned near Rimini. The Assistant Chaplain General was none other than The Reverend Victor Pike, previously Deputy Assistant Chaplain General of 5 Corps, in the First Army in North Africa. We had never met before, and he soon explained to me that he had a most unusual, and new, first time, posting for me. Within 48 hours I was on my way to The Jewish Independent Brigade Group to live at the Field Ambulance, which bore the name 140 (County of London) Field Ambulance, late of the 56th (London) Division, known in turn as The Black Cat Division, a hark back to the tradition of Dick Whittington and his Cat.

Chapter 7

Looking to the Promised Land.......

In 1940, Winston Churchill as Prime Minister, had been asked about the formation of a Jewish Division to represent the Jewish cause which had suffered and was suffering so much from the Hitler regime.

It was reported to me much later, when I joined the Jewish Brigade that in one of his famous 'minutes' Churchill said, in 1940, 'not now'! This was because (so I am told) that even Churchill was not quite sure in 1940 that Britain would win. Certain anyway, was the fact, that if Germany had won a Jewish Division would have very short shrift indeed!

By 1944 the idea of a Jewish formation had been revived, and a Brigade was formed in Palestine with this in mind. The result was three Battalions of the Palestine Regiment, plus Royal Artillery, Royal Signals, RAMC, Military Police and REME, to make up an Independent Brigade Group of about 5000 men. It was commanded by a Regular Officer of the British Army, who was named Brigadier Benjamin. He was Jewish and by training a Royal Engineer. Early in 1945 the Brigade Group arrived in Italy, ready for action. It was said that there were as many as 57 nationalities in the Brigade, made up of Concentration Camp prisoners who had escaped, Jewish volunteers from every corner of the globe, and Jews from Palestine itself.

However, came the day of active service, about 20% had to be found, especially specialists, from British units in Italy. The Field Ambulance, RAMC, for example, was a complete transfer, to be reinforced by Jewish personnel, from 168 Brigade in 56 (London) Division. 168 Brigade had suffered so badly in the Battle for Monte Camino in the Gustav Line, that it had been completely disbanded.

The Commanding Officer of the Field Ambulance, where I was to be attached, by name of Lt. Colonel J N Groves, DSO was a doctor who was best described as a "muscular Christian". He had made very strong representations that as 20% of the whole Brigade were from the UK, nearly all Christians (mostly Church of England), that an extra (Church of England) chaplain be provided, to add to the Brigade's Establishment of three chaplains (all Jewish), and who lived, one in each battalion. Hence my posting, and I was the only Church of England Chaplain to minister to a Jewish Brigade in World War II.

To my amusement and delight, ever since those days, whenever we met, Victor Pike always greeted me as "Hebrew" Evans! We were stationed on the Russi Lateral, very near my last Unit location, and presently the Brigade Group made ready for the Battle of the Crossing of the Senio River. The Field Ambulance moved into a school at Faenza, near Forli, with sub-units nearby. On visiting the various units of the Brigade Group, I found that in the Infantry Battalions, the CO, the RSM, and perhaps one or two other, were the only non-Jewish personnel. The Royal Artillery Field Regiment was about 40% non-Jewish. It turned out that elements of the Regiment were 'descended' from 184 Field Regiment whom I was with in Trawsfyndd in 1942. Elements of that, in turn, came from 146 Field Regiment (Pembrokeshire Yeomanry) which was my local TA unit from home, and I found one or two ex-schoolmates eventually. The Brigade Signal Squadron was very largely Christian, and the Field Ambulance itself settled at about 80% Christian and 20% Jewish.

At this time, on the whole, life was fairly inactive, like a lot of time in the Army—'long periods of intense boredom, and mercifully short periods of intense fear'.

In fact, I was never bored, and the Field Ambulance proved a great base and centre for my work. There were some very keen Christians there, and support for the Chaplain, in whatever he tried to do, was excellent.

The Field Ambulance, 240 strong, deserved a fairly quiet time anyway, because they had a very hectic, nay desperate time, in the Italian Campaign. 56 Division fought a very hard war in Italy and the work of the Field Ambulance had been acknowledged by 1 DSO, 2 MCs, 5 Military Medals, and no less than 14 mentions in Despatches, a very creditable record in relation to the strength. One RAMC orderly, a miner from Ayrshire, had been a conscientious objector, but when directed to the RAMC, came out of the war with two Military Medals, which were not easily earned. The role of the Field Ambulance was to recover the wounded and the sick from any position forward of their location, however dangerous and uncertain. The Ambulances, with Driver and Medical Orderlies played a very gallant part in every theatre of war, and this was recognised by their awards.

(Later on in my life, at the Royal Hospital, Chelsea, I met an In-Pensioner who had no less than three MMs. I believe there was only one other in World War II who had three).

As I have said above, support for the Chaplain was very evident in this Unit, and as always, in the medical and nursing professions there are some very keen church people. This support helped me enormously and I did not feel so isolated. A strange event happened on Good Friday, 1945, when there was a German mortar attack on one of the Battalions. As a result, there were a number of casualties, including fourteen dead, brought into the Field Ambulance. The bodies were decently laid out, documented, and personal effects removed and listed. They were then ready for burial, waiting whilst arrangements were being made by their unit. Presently the Battalion Chaplain (Rabbi) arrived, and was met by the Stretcher Bearer Officer (SBO) (non-medical) and myself. We took him into the room which served as a mortuary, and the first thing the Rabbi asked was whether their personal belongings had been secured. The SBO said 'yes, of course, they are all listed and stored in sandbags'. The Rabbi seemed a bit dubious, so the SBO said "Well, there are the bodies—you go and look for yourself". "Oh no" said the Rabbi "you see, I am not allowed to touch the dead, by the rules of our Faith". Like a flash there came back to me the story of the Good Samaritan, of how the Priest and the Temple Levite had 'passed by' the man who looked as dead on the road from Jerusalem to Jericho. It was not that they were hard-hearted, but because of the strict rules of Judaism they felt prohibited from doing anything. Jesus and his followers knew of these rules very well, which gives the parable a new and more fulfilling meaning.

As the minority element in the Formation, Christians could not expect everything to happen as in a normal unit. For example, there were no Brigade Orders on the Sabbath (Saturday), mail did not arrive on that day, and religious Services were held for the Orthodox Jews. In the Field Ambulance we observed Sunday as Sunday, within the limits of the situation.

Come to May 1945, and the war ended in Italy, for after the Senio crossing there was a sudden collapse of any resistance, and helter skelter retreat across the mighty river Po. Two days later, the war in Europe ended and VE Day (Victory in Europe Day) had arrived after a struggle lasting about 5 1/2 years. This brought a strange sense of

Order of Service of Thanksgiving for the end of World War II used in Italy, on Sunday, 13 May 1945. It shows the Formations signs of Divisions and Brigades in the Theatre of War there.

vacuity for a little time, and it was difficult to visualise that the War was over, at least in Europe.

Within a few days, however, people began to think in terms of leave to the UK as a sort of preliminary, I suppose, to demobilisation. Careful plans had been made, by those responsible at higher formations, and it became clear that release from the Forces was going to be much better organised than after World War I. A system based on Age + Service came into force, with a few wanted urgently by industry etc. being granted an early release.

The global war was not over, and therefore there was no sense of stopping everything at once. Re-deployment, and preparations for the continuance of the war in the Far East affected many people in a variety of ways. Others were diverted to the urgent tasks of the rehabilitation of millions of refugees, and the work of the reconstruction in the war-torn countries of Europe which had suffered so much.

Preparations for final victory had been carefully and discreetly put in hand, and as soon as possible a Service of Thanksgiving for Victory was held at every Centre, Garrison and Location. The Form of Service used was undated, but had been prepared with the Formation Badges of all the Armies, Corps and Units of all the Nations which had fought in the Italian Campaign shown on the Cover Page. My Service took place in a large cinema at Forli, and was a parade attended by all the units nearby. It was a very impressive occasion, long remembered by many present. I felt that I was playing a little part in the expression of relief and thankfulness that day. We were all away from kith and kin, and the background was somewhat unreal, because for many the fact that they had been away for so long coloured their whole image of victory. I can recall one soldier telling me that as a pre-war soldier in a Scots Regiment he had been in India on a seven year tour (as tours then were), due home by exchange of Battalions of the same Regiment about 1935. He did not then wish to return, and was on his second consequentive 7 years when war broke out. When I met him in Italy in 1945 he had been away from Scotland about 17 years!

The 8th Army in Italy was an amalgam of the lst and 8th Armies which had fought in the North African Campaign, and the name of the 8th Army was synonymous with a legendary pride born of many vicissitudes, setbacks, victories seasoned with a gallantry and spirit unequalled in the world at that time. (When the Africa Korps of the German Army was defeated and the conflict ended in North Africa two years before, on the same date, in May 1943, medals were found in a ship at Tunis which had been made for presentation to the intended victorious Africa Korps. I was shown one of the medals in Bone, and there must have been thousands prepared but never issued because the Africa Korps suffered defeat instead).

In common with all units and formation, 're-deployment' was the next 'name of the game', and the problems of peace, as intractable as those of war, soon began to bear in upon everyone. Very soon, the Jewish Independent Brigade Group was moved close to the Austrian Border. Brigade Headquarters was set up at Tarviso, well north of Udine, and the Field Ambulance found itself in a delightful village, a few miles south, named Ugovisa. The Yugoslav border was a few miles to the East, and infiltrators from the Yugoslav Forces were in the village, part of an area which had been in dispute ever since World War 1. Part of our duties was to ease them out (tactfully), and in due course they disappeared from the area. The unit also had the care and supervision of a large Italian hospital nearby, full of German wounded, who were in a very poor state, lacking so much in medical supplies that the bandages were all made of paper.

It was originally intended that the Jewish Brigade should be part of the occupation forces in Austria (78th Divisional Area). However, there was so much tension and harsh treatment towards the thousands of German Prisoners of War who were being moved about (mostly to the south), that the Brigade's move was cancelled, and they were kept out of Austria. The situation was understandable, if not excusable, for the Jews had suffered terrible atrocities at German hands.

They were also suffering great anguish and despair about their relatives in Concentration Camps, so perhaps there was little wonder that the situation was thus. Even though the Brigade Group was not in Austria, the Brigade's transport, and especially the RASC (Transport) Company was extremely active in ferrying displaced Jews down through Italy, to the ports in the south, notably Brindisi and Bari. There they were embarked on craft of all kinds, to be taken to Palestine as "illegal" immigrants, or rightful inheritors of the Promised Land, depending on one's outlook. This was altogether a most difficult time for Britain, which held the mandate, and eventually gave it up.

The Jewish Brigade were a very politically motivated Army formation, in which the will of the Party leader carried more weight than the military figure in charge of organisation and discipline. The Palestine President of the day, Ben Gurion visited the Brigade in Italy, and I was present on one occasion and heard him address the assembled personnel.

Whilst the Brigade was at Tarviso, and the Field Ambulance at Ugovisa, the Mobile Canteen (one per brigade) became static and was set up as a proper canteen at a building in Tarviso, on the first floor, with the Brigade Synagogue established beneath. The canteen was very well run by the Young Men's Christian Association, and I used to visit it a lot. The Manager, from the UK, told me that he kept the YMCA's Sunday evening tradition of Community Hymn Singing, in a side-room, off the Canteen proper. He asked me to take the Concluding Prayers, and I said I would be very pleased to do so.

However, after the first Sunday, I was summoned to Brigade HQ, to be interviewed by the Brigadier. He told me he could not permit the practice, on the grounds that the majority of those using the canteen were Jewish, and that they might think I was trying to proselytise them. I made a strong protest on the grounds that a) the YMCA was entitled to its own tradition and practices b) there was no great "pushing" as it was held in a quiet side-room, and that no one attended unless he wished to do so. I said I would duly report the matter through my own 'channels'. Eventually, the Assistant Chaplain General, Allied Armies in Italy, and the Deputy Assistant Chaplain General from Corps HQ arrived in the area. They went to see the Brigadier first, and when I saw them, the matter had been resolved, with a compromise of sorts. It was agreed that the Hymn Singing could take place, to be conducted by the YMCA Manager himself, and it was not to be advertised outside the building! I was not pleased at the outcome.

Looking back, I fully realise that the decision made was perhaps inevitable. There were political undertones, in the sense that the representation of Jews in the Allied cause was important and significant in due course. No one wanted to upset them at that particular point in their history. Very soon, as it turned out, the British Mandate in Palestine was to face its greatest trials, and within a few years the mandate was surrendered altogether. Fifty years later the

Jewish question is still a very thorny one, and Jewish-Arab confrontations are not yet over. More than once, years later, when in London, I was asked to prepare certificates to the effect that so-and-so was a Baptised Christian, and his passport clear of entries and exits from Arab countries.

I have often recalled the saying 'The Jews have stood at the gravesides of all their persecutors'. History has shewn this to be true, and 50 years after the end of World War 2, Jews have not forgotten what happened during the War years.

Chapter 8

The British Liberation Army (BLA)....

In late July 1945 we were on our way again, and this time the move was a dramatic one. The whole of the Jewish Brigade was moved, from Northern Italy, right across Europe to Belgium. This time the 'Pool of Chaplains' (Italy), did not retain me, and I left Italy with 140 Field Ambulance. The journey took a whole week, and we were lucky in a sense, as it could have taken much longer, due to war damage to bridges and roads all over southern Germany, in particular. It was very pleasant weather, and as we had the Unit's ambulances in the convoy, everyone was able to sleep in reasonable comfort at night.

Our journey took us to the west of our Italian station, and then over the Italian Alps via Austria, Innsbruck, Oberammagau, Munich, through Luxembourg and a slice of France to a site near Tournai in Belgium, where we celebrated V J Day (the end of the war in the Far East) in August 1945.Disbandment and demobilisation were writ large everywhere by now, and it was clear that the life of the Jewish Infantry Brigade Group as such was rapidly coming to an early end. The Group had been moved to the Netherlands for disbandment, and because of the suspect 'blind eye' transportation activities in Italy. The state of Israel (and one can understand their concern in the matter) was uppermost in the mind of all Jewish ranks in the Brigade, and on demobilisation most of them went directly to Palestine by the best means they could manage.

After a few weeks at Tournai, the Field Ambulance was moved, in toto to Amsterdam in Holland, and housed there in the Boor Haven Clinic. This place was a nursing home, used by the Germans as a Maternity Home for German Service Women who had borne "a child for the Fatherland".

There was a large Register left in the clinic which contained details of dozens of girls who had given birth there, and were rewarded with special Home Leave and Promotion.

The Field Ambulance became a static Unit, and was organised to provide medical cover for troops in and around the City, but again our stay was not an over long one. We were moved to Tilburg after about eight weeks, and spent the next few months doing the same thing, this time based on a large civilian hospital run by Dutch nuns.

During my stay at Amsterdam, I took over and was responsible for the English Church in the City. It had been a Chaplaincy for the Anglo-Dutch community for generations. It had been compulsorily closed by the Germans in 1940, because (it was alleged) it would have been the base for an underground movement. Every Sunday whilst I was there (about eight weeks) the Church was packed to the doors by young and old. When I enquired about this from the Churchwarden (Mr Neville Hart of of an old Anglo-Dutch family) he said to me "You have never known invasion in Britain, at least in the sense we have suffered in these last five years! If your churches had been compulsorily closed for five years, you would find them full too!"

The Dutch, who had suffered so much, were kindness itself, and the congregation of Christ Church gave me a fine Delft plate when I left, which I still treasure. Mr Hart took me to his house, more than once, and showed me, in their living room, a tall bookcase, which swung away from the wall, and behind lay a hiding place for the men folk of the family, lest they be taken to Germany, for slave labour in the Reich. Several members of the family had in fact been seized, but they all returned safely.

The lovely YMCA in Amsterdam was very near our billet, and much used by all ranks, staffed by volunteers from among the Dutch people. Near too was the world famous Riks Museum, which was re-opened whilst I was there. There was a full exhibition of its masterpieces, which had been hidden in the Dikes during the occupation. It was mounted in honour of the British Army in their role as liberators of the small but gallant Netherlands people.

Tilburg, in the south, near Eindhoven, was a depressing place, with lots of very obvious poverty and grave shortages. By now the Jewish Brigade, no longer existed, and I was very much in the "Pool of Chaplains" for that area of "Lines of Communications", but still living with my beloved Field Ambulance. Two or three of us were asked to visit a Dutch family on Christmas Day 1945. The family were sad they had little to offer, but gave us a cigar each, with the humorous remark "we know that every Englishman smokes a cigar on Christmas Day!

Chapter 9

British Forces Germany......

Very early in 1946, I received a Posting Order, telling me to report to HQ Guards Division near Cologne in Germany, for duty with The Royal Horse Guards (The Blues). I was given seven days notice, and bid a sad farewell to 140 (County of London) Field Ambulance. They themselves, as a Unit, were about to disband, and very kindly allowed me to take with me the small portable harmonium which had been bought by subscription and Unit funds in Venice in Italy. It had an unusual feature, a transposable key-board which enabled middle "C" to be moved up two places, and down two places—a boon for inadequate organists who found transposing tunes a difficulty.

My "pool" driver and vehicle took me from Holland to Germany and duly delivered me at HQ Guards Division at Bad Godesburg. The Senior Chaplain, the Reverend E F Johnson MC was away on duty, but I was very nicely looked after by the Reverend J E B Cattell, .. from one of the Grenadier Battalions. That same day I was delivered to Bruhl, near Cologne, where my Unit was in billets. From here, next morning, my driver, Private Bob Claxton from the Royal Norfolk Regiment, returned to HQ L of C at Brussels, together with the vehicle. A Coldstream guardsman, who had driven my predecessor at The Blues, was all set to "take me over". In conversation that evening, I learnt a strange thing about my posting.

My predecessor had left on the day of my arrival (no handover), and he had only been told the night before that he was leaving. This struck me as rather odd, and unusual, as I had received seven days notice to go there. Presently I found out the reason. I had never heard of The Blues before my arrival there, never having at that time studied an Army List. During the war they had never appeared by name anywhere, because The Life Guards and The Blues were in the field as 1st and 2nd Household Cavalry Regiments. The two regiments had been through much for six long years. I had seen 1 HCR in Italy—now resorted in Germany, and "each went to his own again". Because of this big reshuffle they were a bit unsettled anyway, but there was more to it than that, so far as the Chaplain was concerned.

For a continuous period of four and half years, the Unit, or the relevant part of it, had received the ministry of a Chaplain who had served them well, "up hill and down dale" in the turmoil of war. He went on release in October 1945, and he was replaced by a worthy man, who joined the Royal Army Chaplains' Department just after the war was ended. He did not really know the Army very well when he came to the Unit, and very little of the "ins and outs" of 1 and 2 HCR. He was a bit "lost", and for this reason, so far as I could tell, he did not settle in very well. Three weeks after his arrival, an approach was made to the Deputy Assistant Chaplain General at 1 Corps, asking that he should be changed. The DACG, give him his due, said he did not change anyone less than three months into his attachment, and that the Chaplain must be given a proper chance to settle in. Anyway, three months to the day of his posting in, the Unit's representative was again at the DACG's door, and the Chaplain left, at the very short notice mentioned above. As there were no families or "encumbrances" at that time, anyone could be moved very quickly. As a result of all this, it fell to me to be posted in as the next Chaplain. I resolved one thing from the very first night, that at all times, I would "be myself" and they could make what they could of me, Welsh accent and all!! I went into breakfast next morning, and sat opposite the CO (a taciturn Cavalry man). He said to me "You are the new Chaplain". I said "Yes, sir" (it should have been "Yes, Colonel" in that Regiment. He then said "Come and see me at 09.00". I duly appeared and after asking my name etc. he said quickly "I see you have been in North Africa and Italy—that will do for us—off you go!!!" He never added anything to those remarks, and so I made my way. As it turned out, seemingly I could do no wrong, and had a very happy posting for nearly a year.

There was excellent support for my Ministry, and everyone was very friendly. We moved as a Unit, very soon afterwards, lock, stock and barrel, to Minden near Iserlohn, to take over from the 10th Hussars (known as "The Shiners").

The barracks were German, purpose-built, and had everything except a Church!! However, there was lots of space, and I soon found a suitable "large upper room". The Chief Clerk at the time was a great churchman, and when I was trying to get things going in the way of furnishings, he said to me "go and ask the Second-in-Command" for some money as a grant. I sat down and counted that I could manage for a start with a few bits of curtaining, for I had the harmonium and plenty of Army Prayer Books. I thought I would manage something for about £10—£15, and duly went to see the Second in Command. I explained what I wanted and asked whether the Unit Fund could loan or advance or gift £10—£15. "My dear Padre" was his reply "we have been going for nearly 300 years, and we are not short of cash. Just get what you want to make a reasonable Church, and bring me the bills". So—I started well—attendances were good and there were one or two candidates for ordination. I took a large weekend party to Church House, Iserlohn, run as a Chaplains' Centre, which had just opened. The visit was a great success in every way, for the Church life of the Regiment. One of the ordination candidates (2nd Lt R O Bowlby) became a life long friend, and retired recently as Bishop of Southwark. In 1966 I went to his Institution as Vicar of Croydon. At the function, there was I from 20 years before as his Chaplain, but also there was his Troop Corporal-of-Horse Muddiman, a prosperous business man in the "rag-trade". Later on, when he was consecrated Bishop of Newcastle at York, I was unable to attend, but Corporal-of-Horse Muddiman was there, all the way from Kent. Later on still, when he became Bishop of Southwark, he invited my Wife and I to the ceremony when he took his seat in the House of Lords. When I met him at the Peers' Entrance, there was a further reunion at the entrance door, for the Door-Keeper of the House of Lords was the Regimental Corporal Major of our time in The Blues—RCM Maxted, none other!! It was a very pleasant and heart-warming reunion.

Life in Germany in 1946 was "heady" to say the least, what with the miseries of the people, thousands of displaced persons and refugees of all sorts, dozens of deserters, and spies of all kinds. One day in my office at The Blues, a Coldsteam Guards Sergeant was shown in with a Polish girl (a displaced person) who spoke no English at all. Through an interpreter, I established that they wished to get married, and so I asked the Sergeant why had come to me, and not the Chaplain of his own Unit. He said something about a clash of personalities, and that the girl lived very near to my Unit location etc. Anyway, I explained the fairly stringent rules and said I would get in touch with his Chaplain. A week later the girl came back on her own, in floods of tears. I hurriedly summoned the interpreter, and then the story all came out. She was pregnant by the Sergeant, who had that morning been arrested by the Military Police at her camp, where he was a deserter in hiding. It also transpired that he had a wife and three children in Birmingham anyway! So much for seeing men from other units in the Germany of those days! It reminded me of the tale of the Officer in Holland who had purloined an AFA43A (Registration of Marriages Form) from a Chaplain's office. He then took it to the family of a Dutch girl he was going to marry bigamously, to impress all concerned in the family that it was all proper and above board. Needless to say, the Chaplain concerned got a "severe reprimand" for laxity over the safe custody of such documents.

In Menden Barracks I came across John, who was a Russian (from the White Russia area) living in the barracks, and working as a cleaner, for a very small wage. He was officially Polish, and had Polish identity documents to escape the clutches of Russian liaison teams who were everywhere picking up their own people. John was very unhappy because he could read neither Polish or German. I sent to London to the British & Foreign Bible Society to ask for a Russian Bible for him. It turned out that only a New Testament was available at that time. I duly gave it to John, who was truly delighted, because there was something he could read in his own tongue and "he had never seen any of the scriptures before". Night after night, afterwards, he would read contentedly and that copy of the Word of God truly found a good home. (In 1993, in Wales, I came across an ex-serviceman who had served with me in North Africa, and he still treasured a pocket New Testament I had given him in 1943). This pleased me greatly.

Besides services at the Regimental Chapel, I took services at a canteen in the town, and also at a lovely Church of Scotland canteen at a place called Wickede. Church life in the regiment was good and my records of Church Services showed very good attendances everywhere. Chaplains were constantly on the move, and everything was very fluid. One thing was right however—transport to get around the Units. New Volkswagens were coming into production and the needs of the occupying forces were quickly met. I still had a 15 cwt truck, and those were the days (for a few months) when I had a brand new Volkswagen as well!!

Great efforts were made at this time of waiting for demobilisation to interest all ranks in a variety of activities. I well recall a great

Rugby seven-a-side competition being organised, open to all units in Germany. Sixteen teams entered and when the final came towards the end of the day, the opposing teams were the host unit, The Blues and the 4th (Llanelli) Battalion of The Welch Regiment. Excitement was evident, and I caught a deal of leg-pull over the idea that these Welshmen could win. The Blues scored first, and then, in high drama, the Welsh supporters sang the Llanelli song "Sospan Fach"—and from that moment it was a walk-over for them. I had to say in the Unit Mess later that to win they had to learn to sing as well as play.

I felt quite exhilarated that the Welsh team won that day, but I remembered too that there were Welshmen in The Blues, in particular two brothers named Evans, excellent players, who came from Neath in Glamorganshire.

A "Dilettante" Club was formed to listen to Classical music. You took your drinking mug along—a bowl of punch was provided—and everyone present enjoyed a great evening. The records (78) were provided by the Squadron Leader of HQ Squadron, the present Marquis of Anglesey.

Leave to the UK was getting well organised by mid 1946, amounting to ten days in the homeland, travelling from Germany being by train to the Hook of Holland, and hence by chartered ferries to Harwich. The trains were in a poor state, with lots of damaged rolling-stock, in some cases windowless. All sorts of individuals could be seen on the leave boats, and on the way to the UK I saw a man from my home town who had disappeared from there before the war, leaving a pile of debts from his tailoring business, and a penniless wife and three children. He was on board the ship, as large as life, as a member of the Control Commission Germany, talking to all and sundry in a most impressive way. I got near to him and he saw and recognised me, and knew that I knew him too. I left the matter till I got home, and on making enquiries found that his wife had established herself as a hairdresser, that the children had done well, and that it was a case of good riddance of bad rubbish, so far as the locality was concerned!!

During my leave in August 1946, I was married to a lady called Peggy Evans, whom I had known for several years, and lived in a village called Llanfihangelararth in what was then the County of Carmarthenshire. She was one of twins, and a little younger than myself. She had another older sister who was also married to a clergyman in her home Diocese of S. David's.

At this time the Chaplains' Department was asking many wartime Chaplains to stay on, and postpone their demobilisation, either by becoming Regular Commission Chaplains for the eventual peacetime establishment, or on a short term basis, for a year or two at a time until things were more settled. I thought a good deal about this, because I felt I now understood well the structured life the Army, was Chaplain to a fine Regiment which supported me well, and I felt I could do a good job if I stayed, I was offered a Regular Commission,but for family reasons, including the death of my step-mother, decided that I should be nearer to things at home. In the end however, I went on demobilisation leave, and by September 1947 was Rector of a small group of country parishes in Gloucestershire. The living was in the gift of the Duke of Beaufort, who had himself been an Officer in The Blues, long before my time. Before my appointment to the living, I had been, since my release, a temporary curate near my Wife's home in the Diocese of S. David's. The situation in the Diocese, which I had left in 1942, was somewhat chaotic, in the sense that (somehow) every post had been filled, even though there were about 60 clergy from the Diocese in the Services. The Bishop and planners had somehow never foreseen the return of their former staff, and there was nothing to offer those who had left from curacies. The Beneficed Clergy retained their rights, in most instances, to return to their former parishes.

If one should point to a weakness of the Church at home during the war, it would be to say that no effort was made to keep in touch with Service Chaplains, at least so far as some dioceses were concerned. The first circular I received from the Diocese was for S David's Day 1945. At interview with the Bishop in October 1946 I was told "I suppose you are like all the others—itching to go, and now itching to get back".

I took this as a somewhat uncalled for remark, and merely said "I am here in my turn"—and could have stayed on as I had, in writing, the offer of a Regular Commission as a Chaplain.

Chapter 10

Civil life again.......

As events turned out, I was demobilised with effect from 10 January 1947, with a 100 days leave from October 1946 to bring me to my discharge date. I was demobilised at York, paid a gratuity of £36, and measured for a dark suit, a concession to Chaplains who would prefer it to a suit of any other colour. As already stated, after a few months in a temporary curacy, I went to Didmarton with Oldbury-on-the Hill and Sopworth, a living in Gloucestershire with about 600 souls.

Didmarton was a typical Cotswold village in the south of Gloucestershire, and Sopworth was in Wiltshire, adjoining village to Didmarton and only a short distance away. In 1947 Didmarton was without drainage or electricity, and a good many of the dwellings were old and in urgent need of modernisation. New housing was very difficult at that time because of severe shortages of materials and consequent Government restrictions. In addition villages were not favoured as residential areas by local authorities, and the expansion of small towns was more popular. Tetbury had a development for 85 houses in prospect, and I discovered that the roads and other services for it were already in hand, and funded by a levy of 1/6 in the pound on the rates. I asked how long this scheme had been going on for, and then made the point that it surely now Tetbury's turn to subsidise village housing. As a result of this argument it was eventually agreed that our village should have 12 new Council Houses built, and I saw the project through in my time there. I have always remembered asking a 12 year old boy, what he liked best about his new home on the estate. He replied, making an arm movement as if pulling a chain "The toilet, Rector".

There were two Churches in the village, the old Medieval one (disused), and a newer Victorian one. In recent years the congregation has gone back to the old Church, after some restoration, and the other has been put to some other purpose. There were quite a number of elderly villagers and one old soldier (Boer War and World War I), who was the clockwinder of the old Church, took his own life eventually by

Chaplains' Centre, Bagshot, Surrey. Intake Course No. 104. August 1952 Staff (5). Ex-service Chaplains recalled (12). New Chaplains (8).

hanging himself from the Clock mechanism. There was a village policeman in those days, a very good all-rounder, and one day he asked me to help him to recover the body of another old man who was found dead in his garden closet. There were two or three other deaths of a similar nature in one or other of the villages during my time. By now, no doubt, lots of modernisation has come along, and times have greatly changed. We were there until July 1952, and our daughters Ann and Ruth were both born in Tetbury, nearby. I was as busy as I could be, and became (unopposed) Rural District Councillor for the parish. On 1 March 1950 I joined the Territorial Army, and became Chaplain (TA) to the Royal Wiltshire Yeomanry. They were a very senior TA Cavalry Regiment with great traditions and a strong sense of loyalty. I went with them to TA camps at Castlemartin in Pembrokeshire (1950) and Stanford in Norfolk (1951). However, the longer I was with them, the more I realised that the army was my way of life. The structured discipline of it all, comradeship and common bond all contributed. At this time the Korean War was on, and several TA Chaplains received invitations to join the Regular Department on Short Service Commissions as Chaplains were in very short supply. The Army at that time was very stretched, with commitments all over the world. Men were still being called up for National Service for two years.

Eventually, in March 1952, I went to the War Office for interview; the Bishop of Gloucester agreed that I should leave his Diocese, and I rejoined RAChD on 15 July 1952. I went to the Chaplains' Department at Bagshot for documentation, and was immediately sent to Dover, in Kent, where the single-handed Senior Chaplain had severe domestic problems as well. My family were immediately accommodated in an Army Quarter and we moved into it in August 1952.

Most of the normal Garrison at Dover, Brigade HQ, and three Battalions were in the Canal Zone in Egypt, but some were expected back very shortly. In October 1952, The Buffs, a County of Kent Regiment, came back to Old Park Barracks in Dover, and at the same time The Royal Inniskilling Fusiliers returned to Dover Castle. The Buffs were my particular part of the Garrison, and very soon I formed a close attachment to them. Their Commanding Officer was one Lt. Colonel J F Connolly DSO, a great characters and a fearless soldier.

He was the finest man manager I ever met in the Army, and had a great 'flair' for dealing with people. When I first met him he said that he would like me to attend his COs Orders every day at 12 noon. This was the formal occasion of each day (when necessary and when possible) and I was to be there unless otherwise occupied elsewhere. He there dealt with petty crime, offered people promotion, dealt with various internal problems which called for his personal decision. Whilst he never explained this to me, I think one reason for my presence was he wished it made clear that justice was seen to be done. He sometimes would defer a matter for me to talk to the individual privately, and I can say is that everyone thought the world of him and his characteristics. His practice was followed by his two successors in my time with the Battalion, and for five years I rarely missed the COs Orders every day.

He was the sort of man who loved to inspire his soldiers in various ways. Once or twice, for example he would promote a man who he knew would not hold the rank very long, through drink or some neglect, and he would say to him on appointment that he would bet him five shillings that he would not hold the job for six months. If accepted he would enter the bet in his pocket book. If the man succeeded he would gladly give him five Shillings. If he failed he would ask him if he would like to give five shillings to the Church collection or some charity. He loved a simple bet with me most weeks. No money changed hands, but whoever lost would swell the collection by five shillings. He was a great commander, loved by everyone. Unfortunately he had tragic news from home in Kenya, for his youngest little girl was burnt to death by her night-dress catching fire from an electric heater in her bedroom.

Church Services were regularly held in a wooden hut Church in Old Park Barracks, and as a family, we were soon made very welcome in the unit. Christmas came and went, and in February 1953 the Battalion was urgently deployed on the north coast of Kent, around Whitstable and Herne Bay, battling with the East Coast Floods of that year which did very serious damage to the Thames Estuary, and resulting, eventually, in the Thames Barrier System now in position at Woolwich.

In March, the 'turbulence' of Army life hit us all good and proper. The Mau-Mau problem broke out in Kenya, and the first unit there by way of reinforcement of law and order, was The Lancashire Fusiliers, who were hurriedly sent down from the Canal Zone. Immediate steps were taken to strengthen the force in Kenya, and it was decided to send out a Brigade HQ and two more Battalions to make a complete Brigade Formation. The lot fell on The Buffs (3rd Foot) and The Devonshire Regiment (11th Foot), together with 39 Brigade from Old Park Barracks. We were sent out in March 1953, with myself as C of E Chaplain attached to The Buffs, and a Methodist Chaplain with The Devonshire Regiment. The CO of The Buffs had been to the War Office for briefing and was told he could have 'carte blanche' so far as attached personnel like cooks, chaplain, medical officer and REME personnel were concerned. So there was no indecision—I went with The Buffs, and my attachment to them was to last five full years, from October 1952 to October 1957, when I finally left them in Germany, at Wuppertal.

Lt-Col John Connolly DSO was posted home, when his tour as Commanding Officer came to an end in Kenya. He was succeeded by Lt-Col H R Grace OBE who was in command for remainder of our tour of Kenya, then in Dover, and his two and a half year tour was completed in Germany. He in turn was succeeded by an old friend of mine who had commanded A Company in Kenya, was 2i/c of The Infantry Junior Leaders' Battalion for a tour, and then returned to Germany for his tour as CO. He was Lt-Col Ernest Edlmann MC, whose time covered the remainder of the stay in Germany, home to Kent, and then on to Aden. I recall with gratitude the support he gave me. When the Powers-that-be visited the Unit formally, he always arranged for a group of his staff to meet the personage. Arranged in a circle, the Chaplain always stood at his immediate right hand.

Chapter 11

On Active Service once more....

I enplaned for Kenya at RAF Lyneham on 30 March 1953 in a Hastings Aircraft which seemed to be full of lightweight clothing, jungle-green in colour. The only other passenger was a Sergeant of the Royal Army Educational Corps, doing his two years in the Army as a National Serviceman. He became a good friend and my organist in Kenya in many a strange location. The trip turned out to be a marathon of disasters, in that every time we landed or took off, there seemed to be engine trouble. We first flew to Tripoli Airfield in Libya, and on arrival we immediately told there would be an eight hour delay before the next stage because of engine trouble.

Eventually we took off, but within 30 minutes we turned back, and all the petrol was being jettisoned in order to achieve a safe landing. After another delay of about eight hours we took off for Khartoum in the Sudan. On arrival there the plane broke down completely. We then had to wait for another, returning empty from Kenya, which was 'turned round' at Khartoum, loaded with all the freight (and ourselves) to go to Kenya as best we might. This delay was 24 hours long, and as we were dressed in British Battle Dress (winter dress for the Army) and Khartoum was about 90°F at that time it was not a pleasant stage of the journey. From Khartoum to Nairobi was about nine hours flight. There was no air conditioning and over the mountains of Uganda we wore oxygen masks at 12000' plus and were pretty weary when we landed at Nairobi Airport. To say we were tired without three nights sleep was to put it mildly. Ten years later I was to fly again in Hastings aircraft from Singapore to Borneo (but that is another story in another chapter).

We stayed for a couple of nights, the complete unit, at Buller Camp, Nairobi, and were then piled into Nairobi City Buses and ferried 200 miles to a place called Thompson's Falls, at the foot of the Aberdare Mountains journeying there via the world famous Rift Valley. We went into a tented camp at a place called Ol-joro-orok, near an Agricultural Research Station.

This camp had been erected for us by a Company from the

Lancashire Fusiliers. We were not very popular with that Unit for many a month, because before nightfall of the day of our arrival, The Buffs managed to burn down quite a large section of the camp. Losses of kit and personal effects were quite considerable. Many persons had not insured their personal effects, and lost such items as cameras. The location of the camp was idyllic, at about 9000' above sea-level, and very near (about four miles) from the Equator. Our knees were far from brown, having come from the fog and ice of Dover, and everyone suffered from the altitude first thing in the morning, when breathing was quite difficult for about an hour.

The Battalion soon settled down to the duties, which began with a series of "showing the flag" expeditions. Motorised columns would penetrate the hinter land in all directions. Stops were made in African villages, the Senior Officer present would visit the Headman; chocolate and sweets given to the children, and some simple military display was usually presented. The township of Thomson's Falls was about six miles away, and the Kenya Settlers in general were overjoyed to see us. There had been several very unpleasant murders and arson attacks in the area, and the idea that the British Army was there to "keep and maintain the peace" was a matter for much rejoicing.

Presently, the role of the Battalion changed and companies and platoons were detached to isolated places in the Aberdare Mountains, from thence to hunt and capture the terrorists who were Kikuyu tribesmen, but on a revolutionary campaign. It proved to be a long and arduous task, destined to last several years in fact. Towards the end of 1953, another complete British Brigade was deployed in the country, and it included the Royal Inniskilling Fusiliers from Dover Garrison, whom we had known well in our time there.

National Service was then in its hey-day, and at any one time there were three or four candidates for ordination, in the Battalion. In fact, I cannot recall that at anytime in five years with The Buffs, that I was without one or more excellent candidates for the Ministry of our Church. One is today a Bishop in London, and three more are Beneficed Clergymen in England. Support for Church Services was very good, and I well recall that when a new church was consecrated at Thompson's Falls, in 1953, I took a large party from the Battalion to the occasion, and they were made very welcome there by white and black worshippers. May 1953 saw the Coronation of Queen Elizabeth II, and it was loyally observed with a special Service and photographs of celebrations of various kinds. There was no television in these days (for those in Africa anyway) and even direct radio transmission was not possible. We got a lot of the details afterwards from newspapers and the World Service of the BBC.

The Battalion was very wide spread at this time, all over the Aberdare mountains, and some very difficult and hazardous operations were being undertaken. Besides the difficulties of the terrain, there were the rainy seasons (November and April each year), all potentially vicious contenders of their own. Battalion Headquarters were moved to Nyeri about October 1953, and deployed around an English Primary School together with a vacant bungalow, known as China Camp. There was a civilian hospital at Nyeri, and casualties were admitted there in emergency. One officer who was accidentally shot in the head was unconscious there for weeks on end, but he is still alive, and I saw him recently in London. A Colour Sergeant died there of chest wounds, and two soldiers were killed in a road accident. I was Chaplain to various other Units around, including an Engineer Regiment which was building and strengthening roads in the area, and the Royal Air Force as well. In all, I buried 14 members of the Forces during our time in Kenya.

A jungle patrol in Kenya in July 1953. Standing next to the bunch of bananas and the local African tracker and guide. A Company of the Buffs.

Nyeri Church in Kenya, where Lord Baden-Powell, the Founder of The Boy Scout Movement is buried.

A Farmhouse veranda in Kenya, prepared for a Service on Coronation Day, June 1953. This was at the location of A Coy, 1st Bn. The Buffs.

Later on, I used to divide my time, and spend some days a month with The Royal Inniskilling Fusiliers who were deployed from Nanyuki, with bases at Embu and Meru, the other side of Mount Kenya. One of the last things I did in Kenya was to bury the Adjutant of the Battalion of the Royal Inniskillings. He died whilst climbing Mount Kenya. The mountain was high (about 17000'), but the climb was not over difficult, except for the fact that the atmosphere became very rarefied at high altitudes. Some people's chests could not cope with this, though otherwise they were perfectly healthy. This young officer was one of those who could not cope with it. He persisted in his aim to climb the mountain, and unfortunately died, the only son of a Service family. He died very near to the top of the mountain, and was buried in Nanyuki Town Cemetery.

Nyeri had a nice church, stone built, and it was a joy and privilege to minister there to all who wished to attend. In the graveyard around the church (very much like an English churchyard), at a spot looking towards Mount Kenya, was the grave of Lord Baden-Powell, Chief Scout of the World. His tombstone has a scouting message on it—A spot surrounded by a circle, which means in the sign language of Scouts—'I have gone home'.

In April 1954 we were all secretly redeployed into Nairobi, at the Duke of York's School, for a large round-up operation designed to screen the Kikuyu tribe and search out terrorists. An amusing story is told of a rich white lady settler who sent her very nice car to the holding camp to collect her Kikuyu cook who had been picked up in the operation as one of the suspects. She was very irate about it all, but was sent a very polite message asking her to arrange to collect her car, as her Kikuyu chauffeur had been detained as a suspect as well!

Many books have been written about the Mau-Mau operations and the emergence of modern Kenya under the then leader, Jomo Kenyatta. Suffice it is for me to say that the author Graham Greene came out to see for himself. He stayed with the Battalion for a few days whilst gathering material for his book on the subject. I believe he gave the Battalion and the Queen's Forces generally a good write-up.

Later on, we redeployed again, around Mount Kenya this time, at a place called Kerugoya. Both The Buffs and The Inniskillings were scattered far and wide, and my ministry became more peripatetic than ever. In October 1954 we received the news that The Buffs and The

Devons, who had come out together in March 1953, would be relieved before the end of the year by other Units. The troopship Georgic (Cunard-White Star line) brought out from the UK the lst Battalion, Kings Own Yorkshire Light Infantry, and 1st Battalion The Rifle Brigade, to replace us in 39 Brigade, and on 2 December 1954, we journeyed down to Kilindindi, near Mombassa, where we embarked for home. My Church equipment, including a portable organ was passed on to a new Chaplain who came out to the Royal Inniskillings. In the event, however, even before we left Kenya, the whole lot was burnt in the Church tent at their location!!

Some weeks before we left Kenya, a Corporal of the Royal Corps of Signals was involved in an incident in Nairobi which culminated in his being Court Martialled and sentenced to five years in gaol, for an armed hold-up of a taxi-driver. He was held in an Army prison in Nakuru in Kenya before being sent home to serve his sentence in a civil prison. I went to see him several times whilst he was awaiting his transfer to the UK, to see what I could do for him. He was from a good home and family in the North of England, and his chief concern was how he could inform his family about what had happened.

He was a single man, of previously very good character, who bitterly regretted what had taken place. His father was a Sea-Captain, away at sea, and his mother and the rest of the family lived at home in.......

There was only one person I knew in that area, a former Ordination candidate of mine, by then ordained and working in a parish across the river from where the Corporal lived. I offered to write to my friend explaining the whole situation, and seeking help to ease the situation before he himself wrote home. He gladly accepted my offer, and my friend was able to visit the family in person and confidence, more than once, for which the Corporal was very grateful indeed.

In the last week or two before we were due to leave Kenya, a National Serviceman in the Battalion, who had been brought up as a member of a religious sect which forbade the carrying of arms, refused to carry out a duty. He should have registered as a conscientious objector, but did not bother to do so. He elected to go to REME, which he thought would mean going to Germany for two years, and where he would never see a shot fired. However, as luck would have it, he was sent to Infantry, and, had he gone to Germany, again nothing would have happened. The Infantry Unit turned out to be a Battalion of The Buffs, on active service in Kenya, and when he was told he would have to go on patrol in the Aberdare Forest, he thought of his situation and refused an order to go.

He was seen by the Commanding Officer, who adjourned the case for 48 hours, during which time he was to see me. I spent many hours with him, not in any way cajoling him to accept the Order, but to explaining to him about the whole business of carrying arms, based on the Bible and the Church's views based on the 39 Articles etc.

At the end of the first day, he decided he would comply, but when we met again, on the next day, he finally decided against.

He was dealt with sympathetically by the Court-Martial, at which I myself appeared to explain the situation. He was sentenced to 28 days Detention and loss of Pay. We were very shortly to move back to the UK, and he served most of the 28 days (24 in fact because of good Conduct Remission), on board the ship. I went to see him every day in the bowels of the ship, and the matter was concluded in the course of our journey home.

Someone, of course, should have found out about his views before he ever came to the Battalion, and he himself should have made his position clear before he was enlisted. There was a dock strike at Liverpool where we disembarked on the 20 December, and the Battalion had to take over the task of unloading the ship. The Customs seemed to be unusually prickly, considering the general chaos that prevailed. When it came to examination of baggage, looking at mine, they decided to ask me to open what I had said was the Church Box, and which was exactly what was stated. I think they were slightly embarrassed when they found it to be exactly so, and never looked at anything else. We proceeded by troop train to Dover the next day, and I went on 28 days disembarkation leave, so as to be home for Christmas, one of the two occasions I was home for that Family Festival in 25 years of service.

Other Christmases were spent together in various stations. The sense of 'family' was always very strong in the Army, especially at the Festive season, and Church services were always very well supported. Many families had relatives to stay, whether at home or overseas, and the three Christmases we spent in Germany were especially memorable, for the German shops and stores were very colourful and festive, remembering as we did that the Christmas tree in Britain was originally a German importation.

On reporting back for duty in January 1955, we settled down to life in Dover Garrison again, but with one eye on the future as we were earmarked for duty in the British Army of the Rhine a few months later. We were given an Army quarter at Broadleas, behind Dover Castle, and the girls went to a little school there, one of the last remaining Army schools (since long closed) in the United Kingdom. It was a hectic period, because the Battalion was due to receive new colours from their Colonel-in-Chief, The King of Denmark, in May of that year. The old Colours were to be laid up in Canterbury Cathedral the next day. Preparations for these ceremonies, together with intensive training, and a high turnover of National Servicemen meant that certain elements of the Battalion were extremely busy. The day for the New Colours Parade was beautiful and everyone enjoyed it all. A small but humorous incident was the fact that the Loyal Toasts to The Queen and The King of Denmark himself, were made after the First Course of the Lunch, because The King of Denmark wished to carry on his practice of chain-smoking all through the rest of the meal.

While the Battalion was at Dover, with the Depot at Canterbury, it was arranged that my "parish" should cover the depot as well as the Battalion. This meant that I was able to see and get to know the intakes on arrival, and be their "guide and mentor" for the whole of their National Service of two years, for my stay with the Battalion was a full, unbroken period of five years. This was very unusual for those times in the Army but it had its value in that many years later I still had strong links with all sorts with the Regiment and its families. In 1981 I officiated at the wedding of a young lady whom I had baptised in Kenya in 1954. In 1983 I baptised her first child, and her second in 1985. I buried her Father in 1985 too, and in 1993 I officiated at the funeral of someone I had first met as a Corporal Clerk in the Orderly Room. There are many other instances, which go to show that the Army Unit/Family arrangements are of great social and spiritual values. I felt that bonds created in the Army in this way were very powerful. To meet people again that I had served with, perhaps after an interval of some years, showed the strength of the contacts made and the consequent memories resuscitated.

Chapter 12

BAOR again......

In July 1955 the 1st Battalion The Buffs moved to Germany, into Wuppertal Garrison, a part of 6 Brigade. It was commanded by Brigadier R E Goodwin, late of The Suffolk Regiment, who ended his military career as Lt General Goodwin, in the post of Military Secretary. Wuyppertal was a compact Military Station of 3 Battalions, with lst Bn The Suffolk Regiment and the lst Bn Royal Ulster Rifles as our neighbours, in adjacent Barracks. The Buffs Mess was a prefabricated building, known to many Chaplains, after my time, as Church House, BAOR. My colleague in the Garrison was The Reverend TW Metcalfe CF, who was Chaplain to The Suffolks. Like Kenya, I had the care of an Irish Battalion besides my own.

Later on, The Suffolks moved to Cyprus, and were followed in Wuppertal by the lst Bn, Royal Irish Fusiliers. I thus had the slightly unusual distinction of having been Chaplain to all three Irish Regiments in turn, and got to know them all very well. As a Welsh speaking Welshman I never served, at any time in my Service, with a Welsh Regiment, which perhaps speaks ill (or well) of the way postings are arranged for Chaplains to the Forces.

Later, during this tour, I had as Commanding Officer of The Buffs, Lt. Colonel ELC Edlmann MC, who had been OC 'A' Company in Kenya, a good friend and supporter in all I tried to do. He kept strictly to the tradition begun by my first CO there, whereby the Chaplain was present (unless on duty elsewhere) at COs Orders every day at 12 noon. I stood to the right-rear of the CO's chair; he valued my presence, and so did the offenders who well understood that I was there to speak for them when I could.

During the whole of my time with the Battalion in BAOR, I was very fortunate in that I found talent to help me in the Church life and worship of the Unit. When interviewing new National Servicemen at The Depot at Canterbury, enlisted for two years in the Army, I met Richard Bosworth. He had no great potential as a marksman, but he could type, and also play a Church organ very well. I asked the Commanding Officer there and then, for the young man to be allotted to me in BAOR, and he readily agreed. Richard Bosworth proved to be an excellent Clerk, Office Keeper, Chapel Orderly and Organist, all in one. With my vehicle, driver and trailer with Church Kit, we could readily take Services anywhere, as we had a portable organ as well for use in the field.

For major occasions the Regimental Band would play, under the leadership of Bandmaster T. Le Maire Sharpe, who was with the Battalion for many years. Later on he was Director of Music, Coldstream Guards, and eventually Director of Music at the Royal Military School of Music at Kneller Hall. He was a very capable musician and together with some members of the Band would help form a choir for Sunday services. Some 20 years later, when I was at Chelsea, Trevor Sharpe's wife died of cancer at The Royal Marsden Hospital in London. I used to visit her there, and I ministered at her funeral and gave the Address in the Service.

Life in Germany was hectic, with large and small Army manoeuvres, Church Houses Courses, a large Garrison of families, complete with school and community activities. The Irish Battalions mentioned above all had their 'characters' in their midst, and one or two stories are worth repeating. Andy McNab was a heavy-weight boxer in The Royal Ulster Rifles, a gentle giant, with a touch of roguery, forthright in speech and manner. One evening (pay night) I was in their Unit Canteen, where there was some fairly steady drinking.

On noticing my arrival, Andy McNab went round all the tables, and said something to all these sitting there. Eventually he came to me,

Ready for a Service 'in the Field' Germany 1956.

and I asked him what it was all about. "Och" he said "they are an idle lot of so-and-sos. I was telling them the Padre was there, and they ought to be in Church on Sunday". "But tell me" I said "how about coming yourself first". "Well" he said, looking ever so solemn "If I come, Sorr, it would give the place a bad name, wouldn't it?" I was highly amused at this remark, and have used the story many times, as also the incident in the next paragraph.

Later on, out on exercises with the other Irish Battalion, The Royal Irish Fusiliers, a very harassed Captain discovered that the exercise, thought to be concluding at mid-day, was to be extended to the late afternoon. All the rations of food provided had been eaten, as they expected to be back in Barracks by 1300. He asked the Colour Sergeant of the Company if there was anything that could be done. "Well, Sorr," he said "I have only got left a few tins of sardines and some Army biscuits, but seeing the Padre is here, perhaps he can do something about it!!!!"

In the late Summer of 1957, The Buffs were ordered back to the United Kingdom, en route for Aden. In spite of more than one approach from the Regiment, the Chaplain General of the day, The Reverend Victor Pike, ruled that it was in my own interest to move on, and that the parting of the ways had come. I saw the Battalion away from Wuppertal Station almost exactly five years to the day when I met them first on disembarkation from Egypt, at Dover in October 1952.

I had seen many ups and downs with them, some good days and some very tragic ones, and I left them with a full heart. This steady, solid English Regiment of "The Men of Kent" (not The Kentish men), were the 3rd of Foot in the Army's lineage, tracing their story back to The Trained Bands of the City of London (1572). They were a very proud, kind, considerate outfit, and I have many happy memories of them.

Fairly soon after they left, I was moved, with my family, to Krefeld, on the Rhine, to join the First Battalion of The Coldstream Guards in 4 Guards Brigade. Their motto was "Nulli Secundus"—"second to none", and they were of the very best. Within a very short time, I felt completely integrated with them. Alas, however, it was but a brief honeymoon period for within about three months, they moved on, from Krefeld to Hubblerath, and I stayed on for their successors in

Krefeld. This turned out to be a Regiment of The Royal Corps of Signals, bearing the title of 2 L of C Signals. Again, they could not have been kinder and more welcoming to a new Chaplain. Here, I may reflect, and say that every Unit I went to, in the whole of my Service, were always most helpful to their Chaplain. At no Garrison or Station was I unhappy or lacking support.

Whether this is due to the "family" spirit of Regiments and Corps of the Army; whether it is because Army Chaplains can go through everything with their flock, I know not, except that there is a definite feeling of cohesion unparalleled in the other Services. A school friend of mine served 27 years as an RAF Chaplain, and in my travels I met him at Seletar (Singapore), Gutersloh in Germany, in Gibraltar, and RAF Halton in the UK. He was very hard working and conscientious, but somewhat uneasy with his lot, because there was a lack of cohesion somewhere, due to the individual posting and movement arrangements which prevailed in the RAF. I discussed this with him more than once, and when I talked to him of service life as I saw it, he was able to see aspects of life in the Army which depended so much on the common cap badge and locality links of regiments.

Chapter 13

Back to the United Kingdom....

I stayed in Krefeld until July 1958, when I was posted back to the UK at the end of my three year tour in BAOR. I duly went to Plymouth in Devon, as Chaplain to The Infantry Junior Leaders' Battalion at Plummer Barracks, Crownhill in the City, no longer in existence. It is an interesting side light on history to recall that a Jewish Battalion was stationed in the Barracks during World War I. Among those who served in it then was Epstein, the well known Sculptor. When I got there in 1958, the Garrison Church in the Barracks was also used by the civilian congregation at Crownhill, who were just about to complete a new Church a short distance away. To mark the link with the Barracks, where they had worshipped for many years, the congregation commissioned a set of 12 small hexagonal windows (showing the faces of the 12 disciples, in stained glass), and the work was designed and completed by Jacob Epstein himself. The Garrison church's own windows involved one to the memory of six band boys (about 14 years of age) of The Hampshire Regiment who were killed in the Troubles in Ireland in 1921, before the Irish Free State was created.

The Infantry Junior Leader Battalion (motto "Deus Vult"—God Willing) were a thousand strong, led by an excellent team of Officers and NCOs. In turn, there were two dedicated Commanding Officers in my time, who gave of their best to the military and moral leadership which the Unit was designed to develop. The first was Lt-Col Christopher Mann OBE MC MA of The Middlesex Regt, who had been a POW in Hong Kong, and met up with his wife on the troopship coming home after their ordeal, neither knowing the other was alive. The second CO was Lt-Col Frank Coutts OBE of The King's Own Scottish Borderers, a son of the Manse, an International Rugby player for Scotland, and after retirement was General Secretary for The Royal British Legion Scotland. He was a stalwart of The Church of Scotland, and told me as such he did not really go much for the Anglican habit of fasting in Lent. However he liked the idea in some ways, and as a pipe-smoker he thought it good to give up his pipe in

Lent, which he did, for the good of both body and soul. I had a period of instruction with every group every week, and years later came across some interesting results. The whole ethos of the Unit was based on the idea of "cast your bread upon the waters, and you will find it after many days." Some of those 15-17 year old did very well indeed in their chosen careers, and when at Chelsea 20 years later I met again one who was by then Commanding Officer of his Regiment. Ten years after leaving the Unit, I was Warden of the Chaplain's Centre at Bagshot, when a portly Corporal of the Royal Military Police came up and introduced himself to me. He said, "You do not remember me, I expect". However, when he gave me his name, I remembered him well as one of the many Juniors who had come from Northern Ireland. He then said "I am married now and have two children. We all go to Church every Sunday—because of one thing you said in a sermon when I was a boy at Plymouth". I had no idea of what I might have said, and he would not tell me, but assured me it was true—"Cast your bread" indeed, in many ways and many places. The generation of Regimental Sergeant Majors in the Regiments of Foot Guards 20 years later were nearly all ex-Juniors from Plymouth days.

"Some fell by the wayside" of course: there was always a big drop out in the first term, at times as many as 20% of the intake, but those who stayed made their mark all right. There were some very able National Servicemen on the staff, including a solicitor whom I got to know well, and a Graduate of the University of Wales who was until recently, Head of S4C, the Welsh TV Channel, after a distinguished career in the BBC. He was Mr Geraint Stanley Jones BA, whose musical talents were of a very special kind, always evident. He was also a producer, and 'Everyman' in Holy Week one year was an outstanding success in the Garrison Church.

In August 1960, the Infantry Junior Leaders' Battalion moved to Oswestry, having been in Plymouth for six years. I always had the feeling that the Unit had never really settled in Plymouth, because its time there was overcast by the Miller Report, the biggest shake-up of Boys Units ever in the British Army. The Report had been written as a result of the investigation into the death of a Junior who had committed suicide (due to bullying). The whole concept of training was revolutionised as a result of that tragedy, throughout the Services generally. As it had happened in Plymouth, the Unit never really settled to its role there afterwards, and the move was of great benefit to all concerned and the future. (The Army has undergone many changes since, and "Options of Change", the latest redeployment in the 1990s makes the future outlook very different again).

The Morality Play 'Everyman', produced at The Garrison Church, Crownhill, Plymouth, for Lent 1960. The Producer Geraint Stanley Jones, is standing to the right of the centre figure.

Chapter 14

Royal Military Academy Sandhurst......

I parted company with The Infantry Junior Leaders' Bn when they left Plymouth, and was posted to The Royal Military Academy Sandhurst at Camberley, Surrey. I was appointed Assistant Chaplain there, and stayed there from August 1960 till August 1962. The station included The Staff College at Camberley as well as its extra wing at Minley Manor nearby.

It was a great experience and I was particularly fortunate in my Senior Chaplains; The Reverend DWA Quinlan for one term, and The Reverend P W Daniels for the rest of my time. The Chapel at Sandhurst is world famous, known as "The Cathedral of The British Army!" During my time there were 1000 cadets, about 20% of whom were cadets seconded from various Armies of countries overseas. They were marshalled by the legendary Academy Sergeant Major John Lord of the Grenadier Guards. He had a most compelling presence, and maintained the tightest standards throughout the Academy.

I have in my personal files a letter from him about a short sermon I preached on the subject of swearing. In it he said that he never allowed it in the Sergeants' Mess, and that the man who swore was "pouring his soul out down a sluice".He was a most polished public speaker, and was the first ever (if only) Warrant Officer to address the whole of the assembled Staff College nearby. When he retired (shortly after my time), the Commandant of the day, Major General Sir George Gordon-Lennox thought his 15 years service there should be marked with some significance. He decided that he would like to raise £2000 from among the cadets (7000) who had trained under him. He would find some more elsewhere to buy him a retirement bungalow. A letter was sent out to all 7000 ex-cadets, and it was strictly laid down that the maximum contribution was to be £1. In the event, the Commandant found he did not need to look for any balance beyond the £2000. The ex-cadets contributed £7000, among them the King of Jordan and the Sultan of Oman.

John Lord was a veteran of the desperate Battle of Arnhem and a

POW in a camp of 17,000 when they were eventually released by the US Forces. Such was his influence that there was a Guard of Honour on the gates when the Americans arrived, complete with Dummy Rifles, and Blancoed white rifle slings. He certainly was a man among men. He lived but a short time in retirement, a name long remembered by those who knew him and served with him. He was confirmed along with a group of cadets, and a regular communicant at the altar in the Chapel, always quiet and unassuming in manner, but nevertheless a giant on the parade ground.

I was a keen cyclist then, as always, and a great believer in family visiting. There were dozens of Army families living around the Academy, part of the community of staff and students of both The Staff College and The Academy. There is a strange reluctance to visit families among Chaplains and Clergy generally, in many places, but I always believed in the old dictum of Canon Peter Green (long before World War 2) which said "A House going Parson makes for a Church going people". This is certainly true of the Services anyway, and I can give many instances of fruitful ministry as a sequence to the practice of meeting people in their homes. In 1956, in BAOR, I went some distance one day to visit the house of an RAEC Major and his German wife. They were not in, as it happened, but I left a card, and they turned up at my Unit Chapel the following Sunday. He said to me "If you have taken the trouble to come to see us at home—it has reminded me of my duty to come to see you here", and he never missed a Sunday Service thereafter.

Again, in BAOR, a new key staff officer at HQ 6 Brigade in Wuppertal arrived in the station on a Friday, and on Saturday I looked in to see him and his family briefly. His Wife was a "daughter of the Manse", and she told me many times, in later years, that I had done very wisely when I went to see them that day—for they became regular worshippers. In 1965, when I was at the Royal Military College of Science at Shrivenham I called at every house along a street of quarters during one afternoon and evening. Later, on my way back, a young major of The Royal Engineers rushed out of his house as I went past and said—"You called here about an hour ago. I want to tell you that I have been married for six years, and no Chaplain has ever been to see us as a family before—Thank You".

The Family—1962
Walter and Peggy Evans, Ann and Ruth.

The Royal Military Memorial Chapel, Sandhurst.

At the Annual Chaplains' Garden Party which I attended (1983), I literally bumped into a man whom I half recognised, as he did me also. He was a lecturer at Sandhurst, still there since my time of over 20 years before. He said, "I remember you well—you used to call around and see us from time to time—no one has ever been since".

I do not make these remarks to be interpreted as a sort of "pat on the back" for myself. I am deadly serious, always have been, about the value of house to house visiting. I will refer to it again later, with reference to my stay in Hereford, when it had a special significance, all of its own. Going back a little, I recall knocking on the door of an Army quarter in Plymouth, occupied by a Major of the Royal Army Ordnance Corps. His (second) wife answered, and greeted me by saying "I do not particularly want to see you, the Chaplain". Nothing dismayed, I asked if I might talk to her for a few minutes. I entered the house, and conversation became relaxed. She had a very bitter first marriage and was "agin everything" so to speak. She said she would never want to come to Church etc. but eventually said she would be very pleased to take a turn at doing Church flowers; she said she would bring her little boy to Sunday School, and encourage her husband to be there—which he duly did.

"Behind every door there lies a problem", has always been a part of my thinking. You will never know or be able to help in any way, unless you know and are known of your sheep, sort of thing. I am reminded here of the tragedy of Aberfan in 1966, which event shocked the nation, and gained sympathy throughout the world. Every imaginable stop was pulled out, at all levels, and everyone descended on the grief of the community—government officials, local authorities, Salvation Army, Red Cross, social workers. Eventually, a serious assessment of the whole tragedy was made, and it had one outstanding conclusion—that the close, very close, community of Aberfan only wanted one thing—for all those people to go away, to leave them in their grief, with their own doctors, nurses and clergy, who knew and loved them all, and understood. Maybe there is a lesson there, and I am certain of one thing, that Chaplains cannot minister effectively to their flocks all over the world, unless they know and are known of them all.

It gave me a great sense of job satisfaction, in every Unit and place where I was stationed. I always tried to be 'known and know', with my own personal motto ever in mind —-'Nothing is too much trouble and everybody is worthwhile.'

Chapter 15

The Mystic East.....

My allotted span at The Royal Military Academy Sandhurst proved to be two years exactly, and I was posted to Far East Land Forces in August 1962. I was selected for duty, initially, at Kluang, Malaya, a smaller Garrison than some, about 80 miles north of the causeway at Singapore. My Wife and I had to make some hard decisions over this posting because we had two girls at boarding school etc, with no one able to look after them in the holidays. In those days children were not flown out and back for each break in the school year. I therefore went to the Far East unaccompanied. In the event, or perhaps because of it, I was moved about quite a bit before my return to the UK. All went well for the first four months or so, until in December 1962, a revolt in the Sultanate of Brunei was signalled. There was a quick re-deployment of troops and everyone else, and three chaplains left Malaya immediately for Brunei. These three qualified for the "Brunei" Clasp to the General Service Medal, for service at that stage. Presently, however, the conflict widened and deepened, and the Clasps were changed to "Borneo" "Malay Peninsula" to mark the difference in the situation. The conflict involved Indonesia and lasted about five years in all, and specialist troops like the SAS had many tours there. I was sent to Brunei in January 1963 and recalled for duty in Singapore itself about three months later. Oddly enough, later on, I was stationed in Hereford and met there the families of two officers of the SAS who had been killed in an air crash in Sarawak, just after my time. In fact, they had slept next to me at Force HQ in a school in Brunei on their first arrival. I knew both of them from that time, though I had little idea of why they were there, and what their role and function would be.

Church House, Singapore, was on Blakang Mati Island, a short trip from Keppel Harbour, Singapore. I was due to take over as Warden of this small Retreat and Rest House in April 1963, from one Stanley Hinton (also unaccompanied), who graduated the same day as myself from S. David's College, Lampeter in 1936. I duly took over from Stanley Hinton, and there is no doubt at all that for idyllic location and general suitability for Christian Leadership Courses, this Church House was in very truth "the fairest of them all". It was sited on the location of the ill starred Coastal Artillery defences of Singapore. The position was built before the War to make Singapore impregnable to attack from the seaward approach.

Unfortunately, none of the massive 9" and 15" guns traversed through a full circle, and they proved useless when the Japanese attacked across the Straits of Singapore, from Malaya. When I was there, the Blockhouses were still complete but the guns themselves had been removed long before. There were, however, four 25 pounder Field Artillery guns just above my lodging, and they had been brought there to provide a saluting battery, used for ceremonial occasions like the Queen's Birthday, and manned by the Singapore Artillery Regiment (Territorial Army) as and when necessary.

They were fired a few times annually before Singapore gained Independence in August 1963, and they were removed before Independence Day itself. Two were mounted at the entrance to the Singapore Artillery Barracks; one was modified to become a demonstrator for practice use, and one, I believe, was sent back to the United Kingdom for historic reasons. Their removal was supervised by Major Tegetmeier Royal Artillery, Training Major of the Regiment, who had himself been made Prisoner of War by the Japanese when he was serving at the very place in the Coast Artillery Regiment. General Sir Reginald Hewetson, who was Commander in Chief Far East Land Forces at the time I was there, came over on a personal visit, all alone except for his ADC, to see the Guns and Gun Positions for the last time, as he was a distinguished Gunner himself.

Transport to the Island of Blakang Mati was provided by launches belonging to 37 (Water Transport) Company, RASC, based on the next door island of Pulau Brani, which lay between Blakang Mati and Singapore Island itself. They were part of my "parish", and I took a service there once a month. They were a very friendly and helpful Unit, and it was a tradition of theirs that when the Warden of the Church House left Blakang Mati for the last time, he was ferried to Keppel Harbour in the Commander-in-Chief's official launch, which duly became a little privilege for me when I left in December 1964.

Malaya was for many years, the main source of tin for the Western World, and after World War II, it was decided that their own tin smelting works should be established, as it duly was, on Pulau Brani. Three or four Malays were sent to Llanelli in Wales, British home of tinplate, to learn the processes there. When I met them in 1963, many years after return, they could count and muster a few phrases in Welsh quite adequately, which was very interesting for me.The main stay of life on Blakang Mati (The Island for the Dead") was the resident Battalion of Gurkhas, in my time, the 2/10 (Princess Mary's Own) Gurkha Rifles. This Unit distinguished itself in the Borneo Campaign, and gained the only VC, awarded to Lance Corporal Rambahadur Limbu, who was later commissioned as a Queen's Gurkha Officer. The British element of the Battalion had their own little Church on the Island, inherited from previous Units stationed there. We had excellent Family Services there on a number of Sundays, as it was possible for me to arrange.

Historically, the Island had a sinister reputation as the placc where the Japanese tortured and killed many POWs, notably Australians, and including a group of Australian Army Nurses. I was never able to verify the facts for certain, but the local Malay inhabitants were always referring to the dark deeds that took place on this "Island for the Dead". Today Blakang Mati has a new name, Sentosa, and it is a high spot of entertainment life in Singapore complete with overhead communications and a casino, amongst other things.

My successor at Kluang did not arrive for some months after I left, and when he did, he too was shipped off to do a stint in Borneo. As a result of this, I "doubled up" for some time, by travelling to Kluang for the weekends to maintain the very well attended Garrison Church there. Church House Courses at Blakang Mati assembled on Monday afternoons and left on Saturday mornings. I used to leave the Church House on Friday evening to catch the Kuala Lumpar Express at 2000 from Singapore. I arrived at Kluang at 2200 and then tumbled into bed. I did what I could in the time available on Saturday and Sunday, returning to Blakang Mati on Mondays on the same train as some of the courses members. Once or twice, by courtesy of 656 Army Air Corps Squadron, stationed at Kluang, I returned by air, (Auster or Beaver aeroplanes or helicopters on training flights). It was a difficult and strenuous time in the "heat of the day", and Kluang Garrison knew this, and helped when they could. Later on in my tour at Blakang Mati I went to Ipoh by civil aircraft to take weekend duties, and more than once went further from Ipoh by road another 40 miles to the Cameron Highlands, which was a rest centre, cool and well above the low lying plains. Looking back now, one wonders how one did it, because of the vast distances and high temperatures. Fortunately, I was never ill, except that I did get a touch of Denghi Fever in Brunei, and slight "transient hypertension" during my second year at Blakang Mati.

My Seniors in the Chaplaincy Services were George Stubbs-Bromley, followed by "Gus" Claxton, who were always very helpful with transport on the main island and other facilities when I had to go over to Singapore on Church House business. One of the things I learnt whilst at Blakang Mati was that no one had ever really grasped the nettle of who was really responsible for administration and discipline and all the other needs of my Unit. This is perhaps well illustrated by what happened at the RC Church House at the other end of the Island of Blakang Mati The RC Warden in charge was non-resident, and various Roman Catholic Chaplains took the courses in turn, on an ad hoc basis. There was a British Staff Sergeant at each of the Church Houses responsible for food and accommodation arrangements etc.

Eventually, the Staff Sergeant at the RC Church House was court martialled for the misappropriation of Army Rations, taking the choice items over to Singapore to dispose of them there in some way. He was duly found guilty, reduced to the rank of Private Soldier, and removed, with my Staff Sergeant, under my supervision, then responsible for both Church Houses. The interesting sequel was that it was the Senior Roman Catholic Chaplain in the Army there, (whose responsibility the RC Church House was, 'in absentia' if you like) who was paraded before the Commander in Chief and "severely reprimanded" for "lack of supervision". It goes back to the basic point, sometimes ignored or misunderstood by some Chaplains, that the Warden, Commanding Officer, call him what you like, was no less responsible because he was a Chaplain and in the long run had to account for everything.

The Commanding Officer of 2/10 Gurkhas,Lt-Col John Fillingham. the Battalion on the island, was always helpful and hospitable to me, as a sort of lone bird on a very small detachment on the island. I became a member of the Battalion Mess and had some wonderful curry lunches on their beach on Sundays. The CO's wife also entertained for me the Director of Military Training on his annual World tour, who made a special point of coming to Blakang Mati to see me. He was my former Commandant at The Royal Military Academy at Sandhurst (General Sir George Gordon-Lennox).

Courses at Church House were very popular, and had a good name throughout the Command. We also provided courses for the RAF Stations when they wished to have them. I well recall that the Assistant Chaplain-in-Chief, RAF, The Reverend Gordon Brigg, bringing courses more than once. I had last seen him in the Army, as my Senior Chaplain in 49 (Polar Bear) Division in the British Army of the Rhine in 1946. He had changed over to the RAF later, and duly made excellent progress therein!!!!

We had Chaplains' Retreats once or twice a year, and visiting lecturers for the other courses, as and when possible. The redoubtable Miss Mollie Rudd, who had spent 40 years in China and Singapore used to come over on Tuesday evenings to speak to the courses. She had been a missionary teaching English in Peking: she was elderly, white-haired, dressed in a blue cassock-wearing elastic sided boots, and using a walking stick. I well recall tough Warrant Officers and Sergeants casting a somewhat disdainful eye on the old lady when she arrived. However, 50 minutes into her lecture, when she was due to finish, they were "begging for more", that she should go on longer. She had in fact been a prisoner both of the Japanese and the Chinese Communists, and suffered a trial from the latter which lasted nine months!!! What she did not know about "brain washing", propaganda, and interrogation was not worth hearing, for she suffered many things as a Christian at their hands. Furthermore, at supper, she would hold forth on all the top teams in football back in the UK, and she was really expert at the game. She made a very valuable contribution to everything—R.I.P.

Chapter 16

The Royal Military College of Science....

I was duly posted home in December 1964, initially as a direct exchange with the Chaplain at The Junior Leaders Regiment, Royal Artillery at Bramcote in Nottinghamshire. In the event, within a fairly short time, this posting was changed, and I was posted instead to The Royal Military College of Science at Shrivenham, near Swindon. I was to replace The Reverend R E Kingston MBE MC, who was due to retire on 14 January 1965. Because of this, my disembarkation leave was extremely short. The handover between my predecessor and myself was minimal, and I arrived in the World of Scientists and Science Degree students at very short notice. It was a very large establishment, the buildings having been erected just before the war as a base for Anti-Aircraft Artillery.

In fact, they never occupied it at all, and by 1965 was long established as the Army's own University, for young Army officers seeking Degrees in Science, together with a small proportion of civilian students as well, who were known there as Shrivenham Scholars. Some of my colleagues as Chaplains, who knew little of the place, described it to me as a place full of clever people who did not necessarily frequent the House of God.

Nothing could be further from the truth is what I would discover. The same proportion of scientific people came to Church there as anywhere else, and it was (and perhaps still is) one of the best postings the Army had to offer. The young,men who were cadets at Sandhurst when I was there (1960-62) were now turning up at Shrivenham to read for degrees in Science and Engineering, and for me it was a great reunion in many ways. Others with about 10 years service came to Shrivenham to study the technical aspects of staff work. In due course they would move on to the Staff College proper at Camberley, next door to Sandhurst itself. I, having known The Staff College very well, used to pull their legs about how hard they would have to work when they got there! (So far as I know, I think I am the only Chaplain who has served at The Staff College and The Royal Military College of Science).

The Church at Shrivenham was in an upper room, a pleasant setting, with a capacity of about 120. It was full on most Sundays, and there was a good Choir, with able singers in it, capable of producing special anthems and other items. In turn there were three organists, a Lieutenant Colonel from the Royal Tank Regiment, a Scientist from Ireland who held a Doctorate in Physics, and a Senior Student who is today a Member of Parliament. Mr Michael Mates MP was a young Lieutenant in the Royal Ulster Rifles when I met him first, ten years before, at Wuppertal in Germany. There was an active Branch of The Officers Christian Union. The Bishop to the Forces at that time (The Rt Reverend Stanley Betts), came each year when I was there, and conducted a weekend study period, which was very down to earth, and very helpful to The Chaplain. The Vicar of the Parish Church at Shrivenham was a good friend and colleague and the Roman Catholic Chaplain was an cx-member of The Royal Army Chaplains' Department, and served together with me at Sandhurst some years before.

My family were of course able to join me at Shrivenham and within about ten days of my being posted in, we were installed in a nice Army Quarter within the grounds of The College of Science. My wife Peggy made some very good friends there and is still in touch with one erstwhile neighbour there, after a period gap of 30 years to the present time. The girls were away at Boarding School at Ashford, Middlesex, which was not too far away, so that we could see them regularly. Altogether, we all enjoyed Shrivenham very much, and have happy memories of our time there.

Chapter 17

"Back to the Depot"...........

The above is a great phrase in Army parlance, and many an old soldier had joyfully finished his time, full of nostalgia, "back at the Depot".

I had been at Shrivenham just exactly two years, when I was sent for by the Chaplain-General of the day J R Youens, who took over from one Ivan Neill in 1966. I had never served with John Youens, and only knew him by sight, so that I really did not know what to expect. Anyway, he told me that he was going to move me to the Chaplains' Depot at Bagshot in Surrey within a month. Perhaps my previous experience as Warden of The Church House at Singapore was relevant. I recall that we moved to Bagshot in February 1967, on the second day of the Chaplain-General's Annual Conference, and that I was pushed straight in "at the deep end" as the saying goes.

The Chaplains' Centre, which acquired the title of 'centre' just when I arrived there, had previously been entitled The Royal Army Chaplains' Training Centre and Depot. It was never an easy place to run, to my mind, and I think that everything that could happen or go wrong, happened during my tour of two and a half years as Warden there. During my very first weekend there, we had to remove to a Salvation Army Hostel at Aldershot a civilian worker who was a sort of kitchen hand/dishwasher, who had become a complete alcoholic, and suffered a good deal from delirium tremens. Next, one of the Army cooks there was charged by the police with indecent conduct towards small boys at Guildford. The Army Catering Corps Centre at Aldershot were very helpful and replaced him immediately, so that he appeared in Court as from his new address. The Sergeant Major, a Warrant Officer Class 2, was mentally ill, and he went to a mental hospital, never to be discharged, so far as I could ascertain.

The first Curator/Librarian, Lt-Col Graeme Crew, late RASC, was appointed at this time, and did a first-rate job on the organisation and expansion of the Museum of Chaplains' work since origins in 1796. The Library was catalogued and completely over-hauled as well. At this time Terence Cuneo, the well-known military artist was commissioned to produce a painting of the presentation of the VC to The Reverend Bayley-Hardy who, at the age of 54, gained the VC, DSO and MC whilst serving in Flanders as Chaplain to the 6th Battalion of The Lincolnshire Regiment, in 1918. He was killed six weeks before his 55th birthday, and only a very short time before the Armistice was declared in November 1918. The ceremony of the presentation of the picture took place during my first year there, and at the same time The Reverend Bayley-Hardy's daughter came over from Dublin and presented her Father's medals to the Centre. The Royal Army Chaplains' Department is proud of the fact that four VCs were earned by Chaplains during its history, and goes to show that the unarmed Chaplain has a meritorious place in the history of the British Army.

A new history of the Royal Army Chaplains' Department was commissioned by the Chaplain-General, and the author was Brigadier Sir John Smyth VC. It was published in 1968, by Mowbrays, whose Chairman at the time was Sir Arthur Bryant, who took a close interest

The Royal Army Chaplains' Dept. Centre at Bagshot, Surrey, used for Courses for all Ranks of the Army Depot and Training Centre for Chaplains. It has own Chapel as a Memorial for the Fallen among Chaplains, and its own Museum, open to the Public by appointment.

in the project. Twenty five years have passed since then, and doubtless the time may soon be with us to publish again, because the history of the Army and its Chaplains is ever an evolving process. Perhaps 1996, the bi-centenary of the formation of the Department, will see such taking place.

RSM Byrne of the 2nd Battalion of The Greenjackets had been selected as Centre Warrant Officer in 1967. The other military person was Sergeant Palmer, of the Royal Corps of Signals, who was assistant to the Warrant Officer and was also there because he was also a competent organist. He was married at the Centre Chapel (by special licence) during my time.

A great day was Palm Sunday 1968 when HM The Queen and HRH The Duke of Edinburgh attended Sunday morning service and formally opened the Museum. It was my daughter Ann's 19th birthday that day, as it happened, and she for one, will always count it as a day to remember.

As adjunct to the Chaplains' Centre was the Women's Royal Army Corps Cadet College in Portsmouth Road, between Bagshot and Camberley. The Warden at Bagshot was Chaplain to the College, though I always thought its proper link up was with The Royal Military Academy at Sandhurst. Indeed, some years after my time, the College was fully integrated with Sandhurst anyway, as things are today. Be that so, the Warden and his deputy of those days held Sunday services at the College, as arranged, and also weekday Communions, Lectures and Pastoral care for all who worked there. The WRAC were a very compact, competent Unit, and the Commandants during my time, Colonels Dorothy Humphry and Rachael Green were very helpful and co-operative. Once a term, the Cadets were invited to come to Sunday Services at Bagshot Park, when they viewed the Centre, used the Memorial Chapel, saw the Museum and had coffee afterwards. On one occasion, when our daughter Ruth was at home from College, she wandered through to the main building at coffee time, from our adjoining Quarter, as she knew some of the Cadets well. The Cadets were in civilian clothes and pretty Sunday hats, and the Commandant said to Peggy, "I wonder who that Cadet is, without her hat, on this occasion". Peggy and I were most amused to explain it wasn't a Cadet at all but our Ruth at home on a Sunday morning! There was much laughter among the young at that. Captain Kate Collins of the Staff was my Chapel Warden at the College, and later on I had the privilege of taking the service at her Marriage to an Officer in the Parachute Regiment. Looking after the Administrative Wing of the College was Captain Nan Burgin (later Robertson) who went on to be a full Colonel, and retired as a Commandant of the main depot of the Corps, at Guildford in Surrey. Today the WRAC is no more, because women in the Army now join up in same way as the men, in various Corps of the Service. The WRAC was formed in 1949, as peacetime successor to the wartime ATS. It celebrated its Jubilee in 1974, including a special service held in London at the Royal Hospital Chelsea where, by then I was the Chaplain, and proud to welcome many familiar faces again. Two women (who disguised themselves as men) and served in the 18th century, died at Chelsea. One of them, Hannah Snell, lies buried at Chelsea in an unmarked grave, and of her was written in The Gentleman's Magazine later: Hannah in breeks behaved so well—That none her softer sex could tell.

On the administrative side, the Warden had to tackle some tricky problems. It had been the custom for some time for a Chaplain from Aldershot to sign the Annual Statistical Check of Stores and Equipment. I felt, as did the signatory, that there were some things which were somehow incorrect, and I decided that a full scale physical check on everything was over due. This was duly arranged from Aldershot Garrison, and a Board of Officers from Blackdown spent a week at Bagshot looking at everything. A complete survey was made, and the results took a lot of sorting out. However, this was obviously the right procedure, and I believe that ever since an Annual Audit has been conducted in this way. To give one example, there were deficiencies of some substance in the "container account" of the Mess, which means that the beer crates (chargeable by the suppliers and credited on return) were very short, due to an extraordinary reason. Some years before central heating had been installed in the House, during a very cold spell, and the installers from a firm of contractors, had burnt a lot of the crates to provide fires to keep themselves warm!! I decided there and then to change the system, and that only canned beer would be available, thus cutting out containers altogether! I believe the bar has been run thus ever since! Just before I left, in August 1969, RSM Byrne had a heart attack and died in the

Administrative Office in the presence of the Deputy Warden, Curator, Administrative Officer and myself. It was a sad, upsetting blow for all concerned, and particularly for his Wife and family. He came from a long line of Byrnes in the 60th Rifles (predecessors of the 2nd Greenjackets), and I was very pleased that I had recommended and obtained the Meritorious Service Medal for him before he died. The Centre was, and I believe, still is, widely known and used by the Army. New Chaplains came there to be documented, initiated with the ways of the Services, and enabled to be kitted out with uniform etc. They were given lectures on various aspects of Army life, and instructed in all sorts of subjects necessary for their work. Since my time changes have been made, and nowadays, Chaplains, Dentists, Doctors, Veterinary Surgeons, Legal Staff, and others with similar direct commissions have all attended four week courses at Sandhurst, to fit them for their work. The Centre is used for day and residential courses for all ranks on leadership, human relations, the need for Faith and Belief in good soldiers, as well as other matters of family welfare, marital problems, and ordination courses for many who wish to be ordained in their churches when they leave the Army. Also in 1968, it was decided by those in authority that all Chaplains, except the Chaplain-General and others which 'the exigencies of the service' so required, would retire at 55. Chaplains lst class (full Colonels) had hitherto, been retired at 58, and this sudden change was deemed unfair by many of my vintage who expected to be considered for service until 58. In other arms of the service, the reductions in age had been achieved over a period of years from 58-57-56-55, so to speak, giving a reasonable period of the assimilation of the changes made. The result of the decision for Chaplains was a sudden "block" in the structure of the Department.

This meant that for those in my age bracket, there was a very short two years left before 55. It was put to me by the Chaplain-General that I could stay on a little extra to make three years at the Centre, and then 18 months somewhere else before 55, or move at two and a half years, i.e. in July 1969. I was offered a choice of almost anywhere, as a last posting, including back to Shrivenham, should I have so desired. I thought a good deal on this, and decided that I would be looking for a parish, and thought that somewhere in Western Command (Chester-Gloucester sort of area) would suit best. As it turned out, there was a vacancy, very much that of a normal Garrison, at Hereford, the home of the SAS, I decided to ask for this posting, and it surprised a good many of my more senior colleagues that I should even contemplate going to a small (one unit) garrison, to a Regiment few had ever heard of, and who were regarded as somewhat 'outside the pale' anyway. (They were to learn differently in due course, when they achieved world-fame initially over the Iranian Embassy siege in 1981!!).

11th June, 1969, Cardiff Castle: H.R.H. The Prince of Wales presents new Colours to the Royal Regiment of Wales, formed on the amalgamation of the Welsh Regiment and the South Wales Borders. The Chaplains present (l. to r.) were the Chaplain-General, the Rev. E. W. Evans, the Rev. G. Y. Bankes (S.C.F.) (R.C.), and the Rev. M. C. Prescott (A.C.G.).

Chapter 18

Who Dares Wins............

This is the motto of the Special Air Service Regiment, and I took the words very much to heart when we left Bagshot in 1969. I felt it was a challenge, as any posting was a challenge, and an opportunity, and I was resolved to do my best there. I had always held the view that Chaplains (of whatever class) were first and foremost priests and pastors to their flocks. Occasionally one would hear from disgruntled Chaplains that such and such a posting was not right for them. There was once a Senior Chaplain (2nd Class) who was sent to a fairly "down town" sort of garrison because his Wife was very ill, and it was conveniently placed for him. He complained because he was not offered a posting "commensurate with my seniority and experience". He was not pleased with the Department and at the Centre one often heard remarks of this nature which were inconsistent with the sense of loyalty and indeed propriety which was called for.

My first Commanding Officer at Hereford was Lt-Col John Slim, son of Viscount Slim of Burma, namely Field Marshal 'Bill' Slim of the 14th Army, the world famous 'Forgotten Army' of the campaign in the Far East of World War 2. The next was Lt-Col 'Johnny' Watts, who eventually became Lieutenant General and Defence Supremo in the Sultanate of Oman. He and his successor were both knighted on the same day in the New Year Honours of 1988. The successor was Lt Colonel Peter de la Billiere, who was 2nd in Command for sometime during my Hereford tour, and became CO shortly before I left for London. When he finally retired after the Gulf War as a full General, he had commanded the Forces in the Falklands, followed by Brecon for Wales, Aldershot for SE England, before Saudi Arabia for the conflict with Saddam Hussein. I found he and his wife Bridget very good supporters of my work as Chaplain in Hereford, for which I have been very grateful.

Reflecting on those points years later, I recall that my Service of 25 years was very unusual (maybe even strange) in that I was never ever placed as Senior Chaplain in a large Garrison, was never Senior

Chaplain of a Division, and only once (at Sandhurst) part of a team of two—my Senior there was a great colleague to me.

Some would say my postings were suitable for 'loners', and this certainly fitted the situation in Hereford. The garrison consisted of 22 SAS, an Ordnance Depot at Moreton-on-Lugg, about five miles outside the City, and the Staff of a Recruiting Office, four in number. There was no other Army Unit within miles. RAF Hereford, also about five miles away, were neighbours, and that is all one could say. It suited the SAS to be on their own, away from everyone else, and the tendency was to leave them alone too, because of their secret ways. I use the word 'loner' here in the less known or less popular meaning of the word. I take it that most people think of a 'loner' as one who shrinks away from his or her fellowbeings, and to whom the word recluse is perhaps applicable. The meaning here is that of a person who either by age, experience or temperament is able to work on his own in isolation, if need be. There are some postings, in the Army in particular, where a Chaplain is away from his colleagues a lot.

For example, a posting in Benbecula in the Outer Hebrides is one where the nearest colleague is a very long way away. It is all governed by the chances of postings, of course, and I can think of a few instances where a Chaplain could have done better in a team situation. Thinking of postings — I speak Welsh, but in 25 years was never posted to a Welsh Regiment, either at home or overseas.

The hutted camp was in a very poor state, hurriedly constructed in preparation for some of the first "militia" soldiers, called up in 1938, at the time of the Munich Crisis. A great rebuild was the talk even before I got there, and in fact the new Stirling Lines were eventually opened by Colonel David Stirling, founder of the SAS, on 30 June 1984.The Church Hut was in a terrible state, like other places there, with several windows broken, and rotting floor boards in several place. I must confess to being somewhat dismayed at this, and my first Sunday's congregation of six. My predecessor had been there six years, and had (understandably, I think) become withdrawn into his shell before he left on retirement. There was a very close-knit air of security everywhere, and I was not briefed by anyone on anything they did, or even where they were at any given time.

I decided that this was a classic case of grass-roots ministry, and that the only way to get through to these strong, self-made and well-motivated characters was by home visiting in a big, thorough, conscientious way. They were a very heavily married regiment, and having counted figures and got lists of a lot of quarters and hirings (and some private dwellings as well), I started. I reckoned I could visit every house about once in 6-8 weeks, and I tried to do just that. I went door-to-door, like the milkman or postman, and left a card if they were not in. I visited the whole community time and time again and it paid off magnificently. I found that a lot of the menfolk were away, usually at very short notice; that the wives and families generally saw the value of the Chaplain's visits, on a regular basis, and there was a great response in Church going. Gradually, there was a thaw in Camp as well, and when the next CO instituted "CO's Prayers" at 08.00 every weekday morning, I just turned up and everyone accepted it. It was a daily briefing on the Regiment's activities, mainly in the Oman at that time, where the SAS were engaged in a long drawn out, nasty, war there, which cost a good many lives.

By now, the Chaplain had won his place, so to speak, and the rapport was very good. Perhaps what helped more than anything else, eventually, was an incident just before Christmas 1970. A fairly high percentage of the Regiment was home, and the CO arranged two whole days of talks to one and all, called "Cross Brief". Every Department was represented, and the Medical Officer and myself were given 20 minutes each, the MO being the first to begin at 08.00 one morning. He ran out of steam at 08.12, and so I had eight minutes extra, before the next speaker, and I made full use of it. No slanging, no Chaplains harangue about Church-going; (one should never blast a captive audience. One of my successors did that on Remembrance Sunday, and he did not last very long afterwards). I just gave a simple resume of what I felt I had tried to achieve since I had been there.

When I had finished, the CO got up, thanked me, and gave the Regiment the news that a very popular young NCO in one of the squadrons had been killed the day before, in the Oman, on a free fall jump. He then said "I am glad the Chaplain has finished his talk—he is to go straight from this room to Tamworth in Staffordshire to break the news to the family". You could have heard a pin drop—they were all stunned at the news—but it also made a point which was never forgotten while I was there—that "EVANS THE CROSS" or "EVANS ABOVE" as they called me, was the man who mattered at that point, and was a vital part of their life and teamwork. My talk was geared to the situation as I then saw it, and as it is now about 25 years since, I cannot recall the detail exactly.

A Lecture which I gave regularly on Selection Courses for the SAS, both whilst at Hereford and afterwards for years as a visiting Lecturer from the Royal Hospital Chelsea, was on the subject of Faith in Captivity. It dealt with the spiritual problems of Prisoners-of-War. I was never a POW myself, but I had met lots of them, in different places and Units. In addition, I did a great deal of reading on the subject, and evolved quite an important, meaningful, lecture on the matter. Captivity, especially in Japanese hands, had taught a lot of men and women that when they had lost everything—contacts, sustenance, medical care, material assets, mail from home, even food, they had to fall back on inner strength if they were to survive at all. Thousands had suffered severely, and many had perished, never to return home. Before my time at Hereford, the SAS had listened to Bishop Leonard Wilson, who came down from Birmingham to talk of his time as Bishop of Singapore, and whose story and exploits are legendary. A film that was made, called The Singapore Story has been shewn to Service men and women throughout the world, making clear that the one who survives depends so much on Faith and Prayer. His talk to the SAS was recorded by the Unit but unfortunately was accidentally erased, and is now lost for ever.

My old CO in The Buffs, Lt Col Edlmann lives near Hereford, and came over once to hear my Lecture. He was a POW from Dunkirk in German hands for five years, and he told me that if the then POWs had received the benefit of talks and discussions on the subject, such as I had tried to give, they would have survived better in Prison Camps.

Many books have been written, many first-hand experiences have been related, and all the POWs I knew have expressed themselves with a humility and sincerity which seems incredible. Among the survivors many have since had life-long sufferings, from stomach disorders in particular, due to lack of treatment for Beri-Beri, Dysentery, and a variety of tropical diseases. Several such were among the Chelsea Pensioners that I knew.

One thing which was not available when I joined 22 SAS was a Regimental Collect. The SAS and various other associated types of units had been provided (during the war I think) with a Regimental

Collect "For the Special Forces". I felt that the SAS by my time deserved their own, and the story of their Collect and the background generally is given at Appendix "A" to this account of my Life and Time as an Army Chaplain. Rough garrison it may have seemed to some eyes, but I was never happier anywhere. Some would have thought; others definitely did think so, that it was a place for a sky-diving, free falling, all systems go sort of Chaplain, but what they needed there (and always will) is a strong base, with an anchor man who knew and was known of one and all. The reason for this is worth noting—as a Regiment they never deployed as one whole unit—they were in "penny packets" really, all over the world, almost as "Heinz variety" in the number of their locations at any one time. It was not viable for a Chaplain to try to find 20 there, 6 here, 10 as individuals some where else. A squadron of say, 80 men, if they went off as one, would be broken down into teams of 4 in any operational situation.

So there I was, at 55 years of age, in Hereford, doing what I could for one and all. In September 1971, the CO and I met on the road in camp one morning, and he said to me "how about going out to "Storm" for a visit (The Sultanate of Oman)? My reply was, I think, very proper when I replied "I have been waiting for 18 months (since he became CO) to be asked to go. "Certainly" I said, and I felt that the complete rapport had been reached. I was the first Chaplain in Hereford ever invited to go to their operational situations, and there were two Squadrons out of four there at the time, so it was well justified.

I duly went on my "trip", like all the rest of the Regiment, and it proved in every way to be a well worth while visit, except for the heat. I was the oldest man out there, by some years, and in the afternoons I just had to lie down, by common consent. I went to all their locations, usually by helicopter or Skyvan, that small workhorse of an aeroplane, which carried everything and everyone everywhere if a landing were possible. I was there about three weeks in all, but just too short to claim the clasp "Oman" for my General Service Medal.

We "remembered" a week early, as it was planned that I should be back in the UK for Remembrance Sunday proper. I stayed the night before our "Remembrance Sunday" at a place called "White City", a position about 6000 feet up on the Jebel, the mountain range nearby. My bed was literally a "bed of stones". I took the Remembrance

Service there very early next morning, at 07.30, before the heat of the day. The SAS were there to a man, quite without any fuss, except for one Troop, about 400 yards away. The Troop Commander had forgotten to tell his men about the Service. This scion of a noble house (he was a Guardsman) came to me after the Service, and apologised profusely for his omission. He asked me if I would take it all again at his location. I was, of course, pleased to do so, and immediately it was over, the mail from home arrived from somewhere, in that mystic, uncertain way that Army mail always has arrived in theatres of war. On opening his mail, the Troop Commander said out loud "Gosh, I have just got my posting back to my Regiment in London." There was an immediate rejoinder from one of the lads, who said, loud and clear "Padre I did not know our prayers could be answered so soon!!!!

That Sunday evening, I took a Service at Regimental HQ for the large number who lived there. I had been during the week before to see the large civilian encampment a few miles away, where the British contractors and others lived, and quite a number of them turned up for the Service.

No one had or needed cash there, and all NAAFI requisites were obtained by signing a sheet of paper for them. The sums due were deducted later, by the Paymaster, from their Service Pay Accounts. I knew this, and produced sheets to be passed round in lieu of a cash collection for the Poppy Fund Appeal. The money simply rolled in, and more was signalled from where I was in the morning, totalling about £200. When I got to the UK, the sheets were handed in to the Pay Office, and in due course I was able to send a good cheque to the Royal British Legion. It was a novel way to do it, and in a style of its own!

The nearest air strip was Salalah, and from hence one day, I was propelled back to Masira Island, where the big aircraft called. I found that my flight to the UK had not been booked, and it was touch and go therefore whether I would get back in time for Remembrance Sunday. However, about midnight a fast plane arrived (Canberra I think); there was plenty of room, and I was on it. We stopped at Akrotiri in Cyprus in the small hours, and there I bought a gallon of sherry, which was the "buy" that everyone got. In due course we arrived at Brize Norton in Oxfordshire. The Customs Officer took one look at the weary Chaplain, and said "OK" and that was it, my last trip overseas in the Army!

I was, as I have said above, 55 years of age, and any further service would be for one year at a time, subject to various health criteria etc. I was duly extended to 56, and in my last period in Hereford, I was acting as Assistant Chaplain General for Western Command at Chester. Commands were being run down and abolished at this time and RAChD was not prepared to post in another Assistant Chaplain General for the remaining months. I used to go to Chester for two days a week (one overnight stay), and did the rest by telephone from Hereford.

There were but few Units in Wales at this time, and they were under my wing, from Hereford. I went to Brecon (HQ Wales District) fairly frequently and twice made a tour from Anglesey to Pembrokeshire and back via Chepstow where we had a large Apprentices College. The Territorial Army has always been strong in Wales, and there were various visits to them as well.

However, time was not on my side in Hereford, and an appointment was offered to me which I could not decline, as Chaplain to The Royal Hospital, Chelsea. For decades Chelsea had been served by an Army Chaplain, sometimes in his last posting. The Reverend L V Headley (ex Far East Prisoner of War) was there until he retired in 1962, when the post was civilianised, and he was invited to stay on for five years. He left in 1967, at the age of 60. His successor came there at 56, and the intention was that he should stay until 65 years of age, in line with other Ministry of Defence posts occupied by ex-Army personnel. He took the option, but in the event left after four and half years, having decided to move elsewhere.

I had extended, in the Army, for one year at a time, whilst at Hereford, and was still a serving Chaplain when I arrived at Chelsea in January 1972. I finally left the Army on my birthday, on the 2nd August 1972, and became a Retired (re-employed) Chaplain for the next nine years, until the Civil Service retiring age of 65.Years later, looking back on my tour at Hereford, and reflecting on my time there, I think of those I knew and worked with. It is a remarkable fact, and worthy of record here, that at this present time (1994), no less than six of the Officers of my time there have reached General rank in the Army. There are alive today three full Generals, two Lieutenant-Generals, and one Major-General, all belted knights, and some of them are still serving on the active List. I cannot think of any other

Regiment with such a record of Service in so short a time, from a unit so small in number too. (The SAS observed the "Golden Jubilee" of it's formation a mere 50 years ago, in 1991).

Did I like the mystique of the SAS? That could be a good question on one of those TV programmes which seem to build so much into so little.

The SAS to me was like any other Unit, once you had understood something of its 'ways and means' and knew how to maintaina silence when necessary. A Chaplain has to win his place wherever he finds himself, as indeed the Medical Officer or other 'attached' person to a unit. The Chaplain represents something basic to men's needs, whatever they are involved in. My task, as I saw it, was to do my best, wherever I found myself, and represent a standard which many forget in their anxiety to be something different and new in their lives. I think the SAS (experienced soldiers, all of them, on entry, not raw recruits) welcomed experience from the Chaplain, or perhaps more so from him. They could not accept incompetence, because the demands on themselves were so high. As one RSM of my time there put it to the CO of the day (after my time), when he said in my presence 'What we expect from the Chaplain, the Doctor, the Paymaster is professional integrity, and we always want that. Never mind other attributes — if they are good at their own job, all is well. If they have any time left over to jump out of parachutes etc., well and good, but competence at their own job comes first. (The RSM in this instance was an RC, but I knew him very well, and we understood each other exactly. Some years later when I was back in a part-time capacity at the SAS, the Officer in charge of Training Wing, (himself an ex-soldier in the SAS) was running an exercise to do with Selection into the SAS over Remembrance Sunday. I arranged with him to appear on the exercise on the afternoon of Remembrance Sunday to hold a short Service in the 'field'. One of the old hand NCOs in charge held forth a bit about what was the Padre doing there interrupting this very important stage. The Service was duly held and a Naval Officer on the course came to me and thanked me particularly, as his best friend had been killed in the Falklands earlier that year, and he wanted a Remembrance for him. What was more interesting to me was that the tough NCO came up too, and said 'I'm sorry, Padre — you were right, you know. That Service should have been held and I was wrong to say what I did.'

Far be it from me to dwell on this. I had my standards, and I kept them as best I could. Others can express their opinions about Chaplains. All I will say is that I was extremely happy at Hereford from August 1969 to January 1972.

There was a sad postscript to my tour at Hereford. Very soon after I left for Chelsea in January 1972, I was asked to take part in the funeral of Major Richard Pirie, always known as The Duke. He commanded B Squadron when out in the Oman, and my 'Bed of Stones' was next to his when I was at 'White City' up on the 6000 feet Jebel on the night before our Remembrance out there. Towards the end of the year he was in France on exercises, and was killed in a motor accident on his way to the airport to return home. His grieving wife and children were at Hereford and the Burial service was held at The Royal Garrison church at Aldershot, as he was originally from the Parachute Regiment, based at Aldershot. I was present at the service and afterwards officiated at a private ceremony at the Crematorium which lies between Guildford and Godalming. He was the second husband of his wife Caroline. Her first husband had also been killed in a mountaineering accident in North Wales. I had known her father for about 20 years, one Major General Dick Craddock of The Buffs.

Chapter 19

The Boys of the Old Brigade..........

The Royal Hospital Chelsea is a unique establishment and there is nothing quite like it anywhere else in the world. I suppose the nearest equivalent is The Hotel Les Invalides in France, which caters for severely injured ex-Servicemen, and in some ways approximates more to The Star and Garter Home at Richmond in Surrey. The French Establishment is a little older than the Royal Hospital Chelsea, and it is, in no doubt, the fact that the inspiration for Chelsea came from the French idea. The legend that Nell Gwyn implored King Charles II to do something for the "old soldiers broken in the wars" just is not true, but a nice, glamorous sort of story of the origins. Much has been said and written about The Royal Hospital, which celebrated its tercentenary in 1982, with many special celebratory events. So, in this account of my career, I will confine myself chiefly to remarks about the Chapel and Chaplains who have been there. At one time there were two Chaplains, and the institution was very much a monastic-style community with Prayers for all every day at 10.00 and 15.00. Some distinguished men have been Chaplains at Chelsea. The Reverend Dr Francis Hare was Second Chaplain there, but away from Chelsea with The Duke of Marlborough during his campaigns in Europe, circa 1704. The most noteworthy Chaplain of all was The Reverend G R Gleig, who was certainly not at the 'end of the line' when he was there. He moved on from Chelsea to be Chaplain-General when the Duke of Wellington was Commander-in Chief. The Royal Army Chaplains' Department owes more than it realises to George Gleig, because it was he who managed to get a proper establishment for Army Chaplains at home and overseas. This meant the end of the evil system whereby civilian Chaplains were recruited and sent to some very unhealthy stations and just left there for years on end, or until they died prematurely.

Gleig was a tremendous scribe, and his writings are worthy of detailed study by any Chaplain who is historically minded, or any Military Historian who seeks more knowledge. What are not seen so often, or known about, are his volumes of sermons to soldiers, which he preached whilst at Chelsea. These sermons are very long by present day standards, but they are eminent, nevertheless.

Army Chaplains have had the care of Chelsea since Gleig's time. Until fairly recently they have been older Chaplains on the Active List, staying usually a reasonable time, except during World War 2 when they changed very rapidly, in keeping with the mobility of the times. OCsF (Officiating Chaplains to the Forces (Church of Scotland, Methodist and Roman Catholic) have served the Hospital from neighbouring civilian churches. The Church of England Chaplain has always been resident, like the rest of the staff, who are all required to live in.

Some of my colleagues, contemporaries at the time of my appointment, said they would not like such a post, with all its implications of sickness and death. I can only speak as I found, and say that I loved every moment of my time there, and exercised a full ministry, to the best of my ability. There are about 400 In-Pensioners in residence at any given time, and when I say 622 passed away during my tenure of nine and a half years, it will be seen that the turnover is of the order of 70 admissions and 70 deaths every year. It calls for a true pastoral ministry, by day and by night, as necessary, and those who think it a sinecure are somewhat mistaken.

There is a lovely Wren Chapel, built as was most of The Royal Hospital, by Sir Christopher Wren himself, who was one of the first Commissioners or Trustees. The seating is arranged as in College Chapels of the older universities. The tradition of the Services is very much '1662 Prayer Book', and it may well (and should) continue thus for a long time. After all, 1662 and 1682 are dates that are very close to each other. Maybe, because of 1662, and the excellent musical tradition of the Chapel, the Sunday congregation is drawn from far and wide, from people who greatly appreciate the privilege of worshipping with, and sharing the friendship of the In-Pensioners and Staff.

The Chapel Organist, at present Mr Ian Curror, who was appointed in 1974, is the fifteenth holder of the post since 1682. Most of the organists have stayed a very long time, living in, with the rest of the Staff. One was Charles Wesley, one of the Wesley family, and another was Dr Charles Burney, Father of the well-known Fanny Burney of the eighteenth century scene. The Guards Bands of the Household Division sometimes play at the Morning Service, each Band once in every year. At present the Choir of 12 voices is composed of professional singers who provide worthy accompaniment to the worship of the Chapel congregation.

About half the Choir were students at various Academies of Music in London, and the others were singers of ability who belonged to Choirs in London and the suburbs, who liked singing Church music. They included a School Headmaster, a Jazz group leader, and a Garage proprietor who sang there for many years. They were very happy as a team in the Royal Hospital, and would come in on weekdays when requested, and possible for them, for Weddings and Memorial services which were held there. When Ian Curror, the Organist had completed 20 years there in 1994, the then Choir decided to mark the occasion with a presentation and a Party after Service one Sunday. They had managed to locate most of the members who had sung there during the previous two decades, and most of them turned up, including one Simon Evans who now sings in Opera in Berlin. They all enjoyed visiting the In-Pensioners Club after Church on Sundays, to have a drink with 'The Boys of the Old Brigade' and they had many friends among them.

It could be said that The Royal Hospital is the biggest geriatric home in the Country, and it has one great feature, absent from so many, if not all, modern equivalents. The Royal Hospital has three resident doctors (normally ex-Army retired), and its own Infirmary, which provides complete medical care, apart from major surgery. The Doctors, when I came to Chelsea in 1972, were the following—Major General (Rtd) Gordon Morrison, who held the old 18th century title of Physician and Surgeon; Brigadier Philip Trimble, Deputy Surgeon, and Colonel Ross Henderson, who was Assistant Surgeon. The second and third named are now deceased. Between them they provided full cover for 24 hours a day, seven days a week. Later on we had Colonel John vere Nicoll as deputy Surgeon, and as our next door neighbour. They were a widely experienced, all-round team, and I worked very harmoniously with them all. The Matrons during my time were Miss Alma Hardy MBE, Lt Col Mary Murphy ARRC and Lt Col Gwen Staines RRC, the last two being ex Queen Alexandra Royal Army Nursing Corps personnel, who also served full careers in the Army. The result is that the sick among the old soldiers never lose touch with their comrades, who walk over (a distance of 300 yards) to see their pals at any time. Friendships built up over as long as 50 years are sustained at Chelsea and I have seen men pass away in the arms of their comrades and fellow soldiers of long long ago.

It is amazing to think how many old links of Service days are held and revived. Sometimes men who have not met since before World War 2 would come across each other at Chelsea, where upon many a story is retold, and many a battle re-fought.

Visitors turn up from all over the world, and I will recall someone turning up in 1972, looking for any Pensioner who had taken part in the Relief of Ladysmith in the Boer War. Mr Allingham, of the Queens Regiment (Surrey), at 93, duly appeared. The visitor said that he had come to thank him, because he (the visitor) and his sister, as small children, were in the siege and grateful to be relieved. There was much wisdom of the 'elder statesman' variety among the Old Boys. I remember that In-Pensioner George Smith, ex Sub-Conductor, RAOC, went down to Blackdown, near Camberley, to the RAOC one year, for Remembrance Sunday. I asked him on the Monday morning, after his return, how he had fared. "It was cold" he said. "It was very cold, Padre, for us all standing around the memorial", "But mind you" he said "It was not as cold for us, as it is for them"—pointing downwards to the ground.

There is one thing which I should have done, and did not do, and that was to keep a detailed diary of all I saw and heard. We all talk history, but we must also remember to make history—for here was and is 'living history', of a sort never to be repeated, and which deserves to be recorded. (I believe that video interviews are now in use, so as to record some of the great events and stories reviewed by those who were actually present to witness them). Early in my time there I met an In-Pensioner who wore a unique medal ribbon. It turned out to be a medal issued by a grateful Italian government to British sailors (he was in the Royal Navy then) at the time of the eruption of the volcano at Messina in Sicily, in 1911, when great damage and loss of life occurred, and the assistance of the Royal Navy was very welcome. I also met an In-Pensioner from the Royal Engineers (Survey), who was part of the team of those who carried out the first proper survey of Trinidad, in the West Indies. He had in his possession a copy of the First Edition of the map produced at the time, in the very early days of the 20th century.

My time, as I try to indicate, was fully occupied, and I went, every day, to the Infirmary, which held 120 beds, as needed. I held a weekly Service there on Fridays, and administered Holy Communion there on Sundays and Holy Days. My practice was to tape record the Chapel Service every Sunday, edit it to a suitable length on Mondays and use the recording in Ward 2 on Wednesdays and The Infirmary on Fridays. (Ward 2 was in the general blocks of the Hospital, lived in by a non-ambulant group who were not really sick, but too infirm to go about). When I went to Chelsea first of all, burials took place at Brookwood Cemetery, about 35 miles outside London. There was a cemetery at Chelsea, but in common with all the old London Cemeteries, had been closed in the mid-19th century due to over-crowding. The Royal Hospital plot at Brookwood is maintained by the Commonwealth War Graves Commission on a repayment basis, complete with Regimental Headstones. Later, in my time, cremations were made an option, and by today, 80% or more of the departed are cremated. The next-of-kin are, of course, free to make alternative arrangements, for either burial or cremation elsewhere, but if the Commissioners of Chelsea make the arrangements, burials take place at Brookwood, and cremated remains are also interred there in the plots arranged as I have said.

I introduced the practice (perhaps not strictly liturgical but not without real significance), whereby the Regimental Collect of the man's Regiment or Corps and the appropriate March were used in the Cremation or Burial Service over the years. I got together a very large number of the Collects and Marches, now disused due to amalgamations and disbandments. So far as the In-Pensioners were concerned, they reflected exactly the Collect and March as it was in their day.

I recall the Burial of a 9th Lancer, and a Trumpeter and small party turned up from the present day 9/12 Lancers. After the Service the young officer pointed out to me that the Collect was not that in use in the 9/12 Lancers. "No" I said, "but we are here today to recall the 9th Lancers as it was in the late In-Pensioner's day."

Though he was not with us in Chelsea for long, I was glad to minister very personally to an elderly Pensioner called J R Richards, a Welshman who came from Llanberis in North Wales. He had won a Distinguished Conduct Medal in the Royal Welch Fusiliers in World War I, and for many years between the Wars had conducted the

Llanberis Silver Band. He was very proud of this achievement, and when in Chelsea he loved to reminisce about it all. He became very frail, was inclined to wonder, and lapse into the Welsh of his boyhood. The Nursing Staff could not make him understand, for example, that it was bedtime, but as soon as I went over, and told him of bedtime in Welsh, there was no difficulty at all. In due course he died, and I was very pleased to be able to conduct parts of the Burial Service in Welsh for the sake of his family present, and to provide for the old Bandmaster the 'March of The Men of Harlech".

A mere detail, some might say, but to me it was very important, and greatly appreciated by "The Boys of The Old Brigade". Time does not stand still at Chelsea, but it goes at it's own pace, and not that of the 'busy world' outside, as glaringly reflected in the Kings Road near by. Some of the In-Pensioners were hardly ever in—some never went out anywhere. There was a wide spectrum of attitudes to life in the place.

'A pipe and a pint' in the Club, was daily, regular, routine for some, and I very easily fell into the practice myself. I went to the Club every day and on Tuesday evenings, in one of the rooms, provided military music on records for an hour or two, which music was much appreciated. I used to visit the Great Hall (Dining Hall) at meal times very frequently, and always on a Friday at tea time. It was always "Fish & Chips" as the main course, and I used to take the odd chip from the trolleys, as they went round, which soon earned me the name of "chip-munk" from the wits among them.

Someone once said that "everyone who lives to be a 100 believes in God". Whilst probably is not a 100% true, by any means, nevertheless there is a lot in it. I shall always remember an old Argyll and Sutherland Highlander of 93 telling me in The Infirmary, where he was a long-stay patient that it was a matter of great regret to him that he had never been baptised. The Scots (and good Christian) Ward Sister, Mrs Peggy Chaffer, brought him in a wheelchair to the Chapel one afternoon and he was duly baptised by me. He died a very grateful Christian not long afterwards. I talked to him once about the legendary military march composer, by name Kenneth Alford, who composed Colonel Bogey, The Thin Red Line, and many other famous marches. Kenneth Alford was a pseudonym, for his real title was F J Ricketts, Major, Director of Music of the Royal Marines where he made his name. My old Pensioner told me how he remembered F J Ricketts as

Bandmaster of The Argyll and Sutherland Highlanders, before he was commissioned into The Royal Marines. Ricketts never forgot his original Regiment, for the "Thin Red Line" has long since been the Regimental March of The Argyll and Sutherland Highlanders, in commemoration of a heroic stand they made long long ago.A highlight of my time in Chelsea was "Songs of Praise" broadcast from the Chapel on Remembrance Sunday 1979. It was produced by Elizabeth Gort, who lived across the road and was herself a regular worshipper at The Chapel. She told me afterwards that the programme got an 'A' grading from the pundits of the BBC at their weekly review of all programmes broadcast. It was certainly a remarkable and very moving broadcast and brought a huge response in mail from the viewers. One lady wrote from Northampton to say she had seen her In-Pensioner Brother on the programme; and that she had lost touch with him for 40 years. My old wartime driver was another who got in touch and we are now in regular contact, as is a former Medical Officer friend who served with me in Kenya in the fifties. Technically, it was a very difficult production, because of the layout of the Chapel—"not to be enterprised not taken in hand unadvisedly" apparently.

Reflecting on Burials and the other 'Occasional Offices' as the Prayer Books put it, I ought to add that whilst Burials were fairly frequent (about 70 a year), Marriages and Baptisms were few by comparison. This is clearly understandable because the younger elements of the population were not present in The Royal Hospital in any great numbers. There were about 20 resident families, but few young children. Baptisms took place in the Chapel occasionally, and some who lived outside but had links with the Royal Hospital were permitted to have children baptised there. Marriages were also few in number. The Chapel was not a Parish Church, and not a licensed building for Marriages; those that did take place were subject to the granting of the Archbishop of Canterbury's Special Licence, allowed under fairly strict rules. Members of Staff as well as ex-members were allowed the privilege of the Chapel, as well as regular members of the congregation on certain conditions. Both our daughters, Ann in 1978 and Ruth in 1993, were married in the Chapel and our Grand-daughter, Rhiannon was baptised there in 1984. The present Chaplain is The Reverend Tom Hiney MC, also an ex-army Chaplain.

There were quite a number of Memorial Services held in the Chapel, held for those with military connections of some sort, and again also for regular members of the congregation. These usually meant large congregations and special arrangements of music etc. Among those who sang there in my time was Kiri Te Kanawa, who was there for a Memorial service for the wife of Lord Ballantrae, one time Governor General of New Zealand, hence the connection. Lady Ballantrae was killed on the road in Scotland when a tree fell on her car during a storm.

Yearly events included special days of significance for Regimental Associations such as Oates Sunday for the 5th Royal Inniskilling Dragoon Guards, held annually on a Sunday as near as possible to S.Patrick's Day, which was Captain Oates' birthday, and also the anniversary of the day when he walked out to his death in a blizzard near the South Pole. The VCs and GCs Annual service was held there, as was a Remembrance Sunday Observance for the South Wales Borderers Association (London Branch) because the Chillianwallah Memorial stood in the grounds to commemorate those lost at that battle in India in 1849, in the 24th of Foot as the Regiment then was.

By the mid-Summer of 1980, I had 12 months left of my appointment as Chaplain at Chelsea. Co-incidentally, the Governor's tenure of six years was to finish at the same time, within the same week in fact. In view of the Ter-Centenary of The Royal Hospital (1682-1982) we were both offered a 12 month extension of our appointments. The Governor wittily declined on the grounds that he would not see the cobwebs and that it might be better for a new broom to sweep through for the great year. I decided to do the same, because by and large, extensions are not always in the "interest of the Service".

And so, the die was cast, and I was to retire on my 65th birthday on 2 August 1981, with The Governor relinquishing his appointment on the 31 July, a couple of days before. Then, in September 1980, on a Sunday afternoon, I had a telephone call from a gentleman outside The Royal Hospital who began by asking "Does the name Gardner-Thorpe mean anything to you?"

"Yes indeed" I said "You were CO of the 5th Battalion, The Buffs (TA), at the time I was Chaplain to the lst Battalion (for five years). I remember you well, coming out to Germany to see us all".

The Choir, the Verger and his staff, with the Chaplain before Sunday Service at The Chapel of The Royal Hospital Chelsea, 1976.

Overall View of Founders Day, Royal Hospital Chelsea, held in June, annually to commemorate King Charles II.

Chapter 20

London's Square Mile...........

Then my caller came to the point. He was going to be Lord Mayor of the City of London from November 1980 to November 1981, and invited me to be his Chaplain for the year. There was something slightly unusual about the offer, if you like, for more often than not, the Lord Mayor designate invites as his Chaplain the Rector of the principal City Church which lies within his Aldermanic Ward. Occasionally, the Vicar of the Parish where the Lord Mayor may live outside the City is invited, but this was certainly the first time that the Chaplain of The Royal Hospital Chelsea was asked to take the appointment. As it turned out, my Lord Mayor lived quite near The Royal Hospital anyway, for he dwelt in a large flat in Cadogan Square.

My first obligation on receiving the kind offer was to ask the permission of the Governor of The Royal Hospital, General Sir Antony Read, and he graciously consented. I then called on Colonel and Alderman Ronald Gardner-Thorpe and said I was much honoured and pleased to accept the appointment. He then explained to me that every Lord Mayor takes a specific theme for his year, and that he was very keen on military matters. He wished to establish close links with The Buffs (the 3rd Regiment of Foot) because they were originally raised in 1572 as Trained Bands of The City of London to go to the Dutch Wars of that time. The Buffs (now part of the Queens and Royal Hampshire Regiment) are one of the few Regiments which have the privilege of marching through the City of London with their Band playing, their Colours flying and their Bayonets fixed.

The Lord Mayor-to-be went on to explain that he was a Roman Catholic, and proposed to appoint a Second, Domestic, Chaplain in due course. He turned out to be Father Wilfrid Tighe of the Brompton Oratory, an ex-Battery Commander of the 5th Medium Regiment which served in Italy in World War 2. As it turned out, his Battery Sergeant Major was a Chelsea Pensioner at that time, and Father Tighe and I became good friends and colleagues in due course.

On the second Saturday in November 1980, we had the Lord Mayor's Show, preceded the day before by the 'Silent Ceremony' in the Guildhall, where the out-going and in-coming Lords Mayor have a hand-over-takeover, without a word spoken between them. The Insignia of the Corporation of London is produced and touched solemnly. Every detail of the ceremonial is carefully worked out, charged as it all is with vast historic significance. Early in the morning of the same day there was a rehearsal (at 6 am) of the ride and route which the Lord Mayor's coach would take on the Saturday. We travelled as far as the Law Courts in The Strand in the fantastic but very uncomfortable 18th Century Coach, suspended with straps above iron-bound wheels.

My Lord Mayor had a lovely, crisp, November day for his inauguration, and I travelled with him in the Coach, together with the Sword-Bearer and the Sergeant-at-Arms, who had with them the Great Sword of the City and the Mace. Later in the year, beginning with the Lord Mayor's Banquet on the first Monday of his year of Office, I took part in many processions, some of them of bewildering length and complexity. The City Marshal led all the processions, sometimes immediately in front of me, and sometimes with a host of dignitaries in between. However, my place at all times was immediately in front of the Sword and Mace.

I attended about 45 Dinners at The Guildhall and Mansion House during that historic year, and my duty was primarily to say Grace before, and after, every Dinner. As far as possible, I used special, different Graces for each occasion. I was told, early in the year, that I was due to preach at St Paul's Cathedral three times during the official year. The first occasion was on the Second Sunday in Lent, the second was on Good Friday, and the third, co-incidentally, was on my birthday and day of retirement from Chelsea, on the 2 August. This last occasion was full of co-incidence. My appointment at The Royal Hospital terminated on that day, so I arranged to preach there for the last time on the Sunday before, which was The Governor's last Sunday as well. Sunday, 2 August, was the Sunday after the wedding of HRH The Prince of Wales and Lady Diana Spencer.

On the wedding day itself, 29 July, I went up very early to the Mansion House, by about 07.30, and was able to see the City in a really happy mood, with people sitting on the pavements everywhere, having a great day out. It was a laughing, happy, City that day, without the unseemly rush which marks the normal days in the City.

The Lord Mayor of London, Colonel and Alderman Sir Ronald Gardner-Thorpe GBE TD in his Coach on Lord Mayor's Day 1980.

As Chaplain to the Lord Mayor, I was present at the wedding, in the Chancel, beneath the Lord Mayor's Stall, for the marriage itself. The Lord Mayor carried the Great Sword himself that day, in and out of St Paul's Cathedral, immediately before The Sovereign.

On the Sunday following,(my 65th birthday) when I preached at St Paul's, there was a vast congregation. The Cathedral was full, and it was of no use my fondly thinking they were there to hear me. Most of them were there to catch something of the spirit of the previous Wednesday, and to see the flowers, which were still in place!

Altogether, it was a remarkable year, and though I left London in August 1981, I commuted to various functions until November, and thoroughly enjoyed the honour of my Chaplaincy. Before the end of the year, I and my co-Chaplain, Father Tighe, were made Freemen of the City.

In December 1991 Ronald Gardner-Thorpe died and in March 1992 I participated in his Memorial Service at The Church of S. Lawrence Jewry, next Guildhall, the Corporation of the City's of London's own Church.

Chapter 21

Move to Swansea and Retirement........

We had bought a house in Swansea some years before, and had let it to students at Swansea University, for a year at a time, as it was too far away for us to use it as a retreat. We duly went there in August 1981, but I was still not finished with my connections with the Army. There had been no Army Chaplain with the SAS at Hereford for some time, and the CO of the day in 1981 (now General Sir Michael Rose, Adjutant General in his present Army appointment), made urgent representations that I should return on a part-time basis to Hereford. In Army parlance I was an OCF (B), (Officiating Chaplain to the Forces (Grade B). Swansea was 75 miles away from Hereford, but I agreed to undertake the task for the time being, with the promise that an Army Chaplain would take over presently. In the event, it was 18 months before a new Senior Chaplain (Wales) was organised to be responsible for Hereford Garrison.

It is one of the lessons of life that things are never the same the second time round, and this was true of Hereford Garrison, for a variety of reasons. In the first place, I felt very much that I was not able to give the task my whole attention because of the distances involved. I aimed to be there three times a month; once for a weekend for a Sunday when there was the monthly Service in the Garrison Church. (When I was there before, from 1969-1972, two Services were held every Sunday). I also went to Hereford for three days a week twice in the month, which was really quite inadequate for the task of being Chaplain and friend to all.

As always in the past, there was carte-blanche for me to go everywhere, see everything and everyone. A lot of the old faces of my previous time there—some very good friends among them—had moved up in the Service, and had done very well. Bradbury Lines, originally named after a Royal Artillery VC of World War I, was in the process of being completely rebuilt, to replace the hutted camp built in 1938 for the use of some of the first Militia men, called up when World War 2 was threatening. It was to receive the new name of

Stirling Lines, to commemorate David Stirling, the founder of the SAS in the Middle East in 1941.

The day I arrived as a part-time Chaplain I was sent off immediately to Bristol to see the parents of young trainee officer, about to join the Regiment, who had been killed accidentally on jungle training in Guyana. He was a very clever young man, a Law Graduate of his University, the delight of his parents, and it was all very sad.

In May 1982, my Wife and I went for a week's holiday to Sorrento in Italy (I was last there in 1944). Whilst on this holiday, my only Brother died very tragically in Cheshire.Our flight home was delayed by an Air Traffic Controller strike in Italy, and we finally landed at 06.00 on a Friday morning. After a short break in London, we drove that day to Henbury, near Macclesfield for my Brother's funeral next day. On that same day the news broke of the loss of 18 lives in a helicopter crash in the Falklands War. No direct reference was made to the SAS, but I at once recognised two of the names given, and knew that Hereford was in trouble.

On the next day, Sunday, we travelled back to Swansea, via Hereford. I saw the Station Staff Officer there, Major Peter Davey, (an old colleague), and said I would return the next day, which I duly did. I spent the whole week there doing what I could among the bereaved, and found that I knew well most of those lost. Looking back since, I yearned for the relationship established in 1969-1972 when I knew every family very well, and was a familiar face to them all. In the years between, because of the absence of a regular Chaplain in their midst, some families had got to dread the spectacle of the Station Staff Officer and a clergyman of any kind in the area of the Quarters—it was the harbinger of bad news for someone, and they all knew it.

Various Memorial Services were held, some at the Parish Church nearby, where the SAS had their dead buried. A year to the day of this major disaster in the Falklands, I preached at St. Martin's Parish Church, when a Memorial Window, Pews and Book of Remembrance were dedicated by the Lord Bishop of Hereford. It was a grave, moving, occasion and my Address was based on the Regiment's abbreviated title Sacrifice, Appreciation, Sanctification—SAS.

Already the Senior Chaplain from HQ Wales had taken over, but I was there for the dedication of the new Garrison Church of St. Christopher in September 1983. Hereford was yet again, very shortly, to be bereft of a Chaplain because by Remembrance tide of that year, the Senior Chaplain's Wife was very ill with a terminal illness, and he was withdrawn. However, by now, I felt I could not effectively do much more, and thought I ought not begin yet again, at the distance I was from it all.I really came face to face with full retirement at this time and plunged into the task of acquiring, arranging for major improvements, and adaptation of the house we are now in at Llandysul, in Dyfed, where we moved to in April 1985. Since then, like most retired Clergy, I have been used pretty constantly in taking Services in vacant parishes around, Sunday by Sunday (together with weddings and funerals of family and friends, membership of The Royal British Legion, lectures on The Royal Hospital etc. etc.).

Llandysul itself provided one or two surprises as we got to know the village and its inhabitants. The Porth Hotel, the hostelry next door to the Parish Church gave my wife and I a nice reminder when we visited there one day. In the bar there was an interesting picture on the wall which turned out to be a print of a Collage, executed in 1981, showing a cricket match in progress at Burton Court, just across the road from the Royal Hospital in Chelsea. In the background was the main building of the Royal Hospital, showing the Wren Chapel and Dining Hall, on Burton Court the Band of The Coldstream Guards was playing, all very well known to me; there were In-Pensioner spectators at the match, and the whole was beautifully executed. The Collage had been bought by Mr and Mrs James, mine hosts of the Porth Hotel, at a craft centre in Llandysul. I wished I could have bought it myself, for it portrayed so much of what we had known as a family in London for a decade.

A surprise in Llandysul was to meet again Dr John Cule MD and his wife Mrs Leslie Cule. He was in a practice in Camberley, when we were stationed at Sandhurst in 1960. He was learning Welsh at the time, and he and I spent many an hour conning the Welsh pages in a Cardiganshire Weekly, the Welsh Gazette. Dr Cule is now living in retirement near Llandysul, and he is a well-known authority on the History of Medicine. He lectures on many aspects of this subject and many kindred matters in many places, both at home and abroad. In 1985, the year in which we came to live in Llandysul, he was made High Sheriff of Dyfed, and he did me the signal honour of appointing me as his Chaplain for the year. He wittily said to me 'You have had a little experience of this office during your year with the Lord Mayor of London! We attended several sessions of Crown Courts at Carmarthen and Haverfordwest during the year. Regrettably Crown Courts are no longer held at Lampeter where I attended the Assizes many times as a youth and student at S. David's College before World War 2. We paid an official visit to the Army Headquarters known as HQ Wales District and were entertained to lunch by the General Officer Commanding who was none other than Major General (now General Sir Peter de la Billiere) of long association since we were together at 22 SAS. Another Llandysul co-incidence was to meet again Captain James Lunn whom I had first met as a very young officer in 1954, when he arrived in Kenya to join The Buffs. He was invalided out of the Army over an explosion which damaged his hearing, and has since had a very good career in Personnel. Now retired, he comes regularly to fish the Teifi, and recently had our old Commanding Officer, Lt-Col Ernest Edlmann, as his guest on the river.

Two old comrades of the SAS live in the area, and I see one of them fairly frequently shopping in the village. The other was a Warrant Officer responsible for stores (RQMS). When I sent out to the Oman I was asked to look after two wooden boxes on the journey. I nearly lost one of them in Cyprus, through no fault of my own, but got them out there safely in the end, after a journey which took five days to complete. They turned out to be night-sights for extra vision in the dark, and the RQMS sent a signal (Army message) back to base as follows "Evans Above has brought us light in our darkness".

Llandysul itself has lots of history and interest. It is built on the banks of the river Teifi, and most of the housing is located on the slopes of the steep hillside arising from the valley and has a population of 2,000. The Parish Church is largely 13th century, and has interesting features including the Velvor Stone which goes back to Roman times. It is well known for its religious festival known as Calan Hen (Old New Year), now celebrated with a day long Sunday School Festival of Bible Recitation, questions on selected passages, Anthems etc., and is continuous from 10.30 until completed by about a dozen Schools from neighbouring parishes. For generations this day was marked by a large scale football match of terrifying proportions and rough play. The goal posts were the porches of the Parish Churches of Llandysul and Llanwenog, about five miles apart. About

The High Sheriff of Dyfed Dr John Cule MD, and his Chaplain on Installation Day, 29 March 1985.

150 years ago the then Vicar, the Reverend Enoch James called a halt to the carnage and started the Festival instead, and this has gone on from strength every since.

In September 1995 the local secondary School celebrated its centenary, and the School too is marked by some unusual history. In 1890 plans were formulated to provide formal secondary education for the children of the County (Cardiganshire), schools to be built in certain places. Llandysul was not included, and this so aroused the fury of the inhabitants that public meetings were held, and money raised to accompany a petition to the LEA. There were sufficient funds produced there and then to build a complete school. The result was it was completed before any other of the planned schools. In 1923 the Burnham Scale of pay was produced for Teachers nation-wide, but the only authority which refused to implement it was Cardiganshire. There was a Teachers' strike, certain "black-leg" teachers were recruited, and those who were suspended had their pay made up by the NUT until they retired, many years later.

A history of the first 100 years was produced for the centenary, and a 1000 copies were produced. Such was the interest taken that 900 copies were sold within seven days. The book was produced by Mr

Arwyn Pierce, prior Headmaster to the present Head, Mr Ainsleigh Davies. The School in its early years was taught entirely in English, but in 1965 became a fully bi-lingual School. My wife was a pupil of the School in the early thirties, and what amazes me more than anything is to note what talent the School produced over the decades. Scores of pupils became professional men and women. On of the most illustrious became Professor of Physics at Aberystwyth University College. His name was E J Williams and he was Churchill's chief adviser on devices for anti-submarine warfare in the dark days of the war of 1939-45. The story goes that he was urgently summoned from his home to Downing Street on one occasion, and was booked for speeding by nearly every police force on the way! Unfortunately he died at a very early age after the war, a brilliant pupil of the School, from a very humble background in Cardiganshire.

Today the village is centred on tourism, agriculture, fishing in the river, a very modern and progressive Book Publisher, Gomer Press, also a 100 years old about the same time. Welsh is the predominant language today, and the local MP is a member of the Welsh Nationalist Party.

Chapter 22

The Last Word..............

During my time then, since 1942, I have held every type of appointment the Royal Army Chaplains' Department can offer, with all its various types of Commissions, except that of Section B (Cadets) in the Territorial Army. I have been very content with my lot, blessed with good health for all my Service, and made a host of friends in many situations and circumstances. I express my gratitude for all the opportunities that came my way, and hope that not too many were missed or neglected.

LAUS DEO

The Chapel of The Royal Hospital Chelsea, part of the Sir Christopher Wren design for the whole complex. Built 1682-1692.

APPENDIX 1

The Regimental Collects of The British Army......

In 1930 a Book was published in Plymouth called "Collects of The British Army" over the name of The Reverend Matthew Tobias, Chaplain to the Forces, and also Chaplain to The Royal Hospital Chelsea, at the end of his military career. He says in the preface to his book that he got the original idea from The Reverend Christopher Milner, Vicar of Warden with Newborough, near Hexham, Northumberland, who was a Chaplain in the Territorial Army. He had produced a small number of Collects for various Regiments, originally for use in the Diocese of Newcastle.

Matthew Tobias followed up this idea, and his book was a very well produced volume, covering all Regiments and Corps of the Army in his day. By now, of course, disbandments, amalgamations and changes galore have altered many units beyond recognition, but Tobias' work is historic and fascinating for the way in which the Prayers were constructed. Each Collect appears on a page opposite a drawing of the Regimental or Corps Badge, underneath which are listed the Battle Honours of the Unit. On the other page is the text of the Collect with Biblical and Regimental footnotes to match. I give below one example from the Book, the Collect of the Royal Army Chaplains' Department. The Badge (as approved in 1919, after World War I, when the Department became "Royal" in its title, shows a Maltese Cross upon a wreath of laurel and oak leaves. In the centre, a quatrefoil voided within a circle inscribed with the motto "In this sign conquer". The whole is ensign with the Imperial Crown.

The Collect reads as follows:-

Blessed Lord, who hast committed the glorious gospel to our trust (1), have mercy on the Royal Army Chaplains' Department, and grant that we may never glory save in the Cross of our Lord Jesus Christ (2), but in all things may approve ourselves as thy Ministers (3), lest this Cross be made of none effect (4); through the same Jesus Christ our Lord.

Amen

Footnotes

1. 1 Timothy 1 verse 11: "The glorious gospel of the blessed God, which was committed to my trust"

2. (a) Galatians 6 verse 14 "God forbid that I should glory save in the Cross of our Lord, Jesus Christ".

(b) Motto of the Department: "In this sign conquer".

3. 2 Corinthians 6 verse 4: "In all things approving ourselves as the Ministers of God".

4. 1 Corinthians 1 verse 17: "Christ sent me .... to preach the gospel; not with wisdom of words, lest the Cross of Christ be made of none effect"

2 and 4. Badge of the Department: A Maltese Cross

The example I have given is used today exactly as originally composed by Matthew Tobias. Some Collects have been amended or modernised to meet the needs of amalgamations of Regiments etc. and there are several new ones in the course of the years since 1930. When I was Warden at the Centre at Bagshot, a new collection was published by the Chaplain-General, and given the approval of the Army Council, now the Army Board. Some of the additions do not have footnotes, neither does the book include the Regimental and Corps Badges which in many instances provide some of the inspiration of the words of the text of the Collect.

When I arrived at 22 SAS in August 1969 I found there was no Regimental Collect as such, and I took it upon myself to provide one. It is now approved for Regimental use, and goes as follows:-

O Lord, who didst call on thy disciples to venture all to win all men to thee, grant that we, the chosen members of the Special Air Service Regiment, may by our work and our ways dare all to win all, and in so doing render Special Service to Thee and our fellow-men in all the world, through the same Jesus Christ our Lord. AMEN.

It was produced in Book-mark form, but in true SAS usage had to be memorised by those who wished to use it, because to carry it around might create a breach of their own security measures. Many copies, of course, can be found in the homes of those who served in the Regiment at any time.

Appendix 2

List of Regiments, Units and Garrisons served with......

Wartime Service

184 Field Regiment, Royal Artillery	UK Sept 42- Jan 43
79 (Herts Yeomanry) Heavy Anti-Aircraft Royal Artillery	North Africa Jan 43 Italy - Jan 45
56 Heavy Regiment, Royal Artillery	Italy Jan 45 - March 45
The Jewish Independent Brigade Group	Italy March 45 Belgium- Holland Jan 46
Royal Horse Guards (The Blues)	Germany Jan 46 - Jan 47

Territorial Army

Royal Wiltshire Yeomanry (TA)	UK March 50 - July 52

Regular Army

1 Bn The Buffs (Royal East Kent Regiment)	UK July 52 Kenya,UK- Germany Oct 57
HQ 6 Infantry Brigade	Germany Oct 57 - Dec 57
1 Bn Coldstream Guards	Germany Dec 57 - Mar 58
2 L of C Regiment, Royal Signals	Germany Mar 58— July 58
Infantry Junior Leaders' Battalion	Plymouth July 58 - July 60
Royal Military Academy Sandhurst	Camberley July 60 - July 62
Kluang Garrison	Malaya Aug 62 - Jan 63
HQ 99 Gurkha Infantry Brigade	Borneo Jan 63 - March 63
Warden Church House Farelf	Singapore Mar 63 - Dec 64

Royal Military College of Science
Shrivenham, Wiltshire UK Dec 64 -
Feb 67
Warden RAChD Centre, Bagshot, Surrey UK Feb 67 -
Aug 69
22 SAS Regiment and Senior Chaplain Wales UK Aug 69 -
Jan 72
Royal Hospital Chelsea, London UK Jan 72 -
Aug 81
(Retired Chaplain—Reemployed from August 72—August 81)
Retired
Part-time Chaplain to 22 SAS Regiment during the Falklands War

REFERENCES

Allen, C	The Savage Wars of Peace	Michael Joseph 1990
De La Billiere, P	Storm Command	Harper Collins 1990
De La Billiere, P	Looking for Trouble	Harper Collins 1994
Blaxland, G	The Buffs 1948-67	Queen's Own Buffs 1967
Dean, C	The Royal Hospital, Chelsea 1681-1950	Hutchinson 1950
Dickens, P	The Jungle Frontier (Borneo 1963-66)	Arms and Armour Press 1983
Hackett, J	The Profession of Arms	Sidgwick and Jackson 1983
Hart, J	History of The Second World War	Cassell 1970
Linklater, E	The Campaign in Italy	HMSO 1977
Lloyd Thomas J R	Moth or Phoenix	Gomer Press 1980
Morris, J	Sultan in Oman	Weidenfeld &Nicolson 1961
Smyth, J	Sandhurst	Weidenfeld & Nicholson 1961
Smyth, J	In this sign conquer	Mowbrays 1968
Swinson, A	A Register of the Regiments & Corps of the British Army	Archive Press 1972
Tobias, M	Regimental Collects of The British Army	Underhill 1930
Warner, P	SAS—The Offical History	Sphere 1983